ARCTIC

FOREST

NORTHEAST
WOODLANDS

NORTH

ATLANTIC

COAST

GREAT LAKES

MERICAN

PRAIRIE

APPALACHIAN
HIGHLANDS

SOUTH
ATLANTIC
COAST
AND
PIEDMONT

SOUTHERN
HILL
COUNTRY

GULF COAST

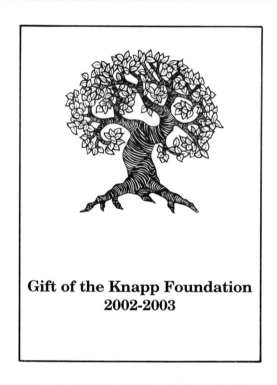

The *Stories from Where We Live* Series

Each volume in the *Stories from Where We Live* series celebrates a North American ecoregion through its own distinctive literature. For thousands of years, people have told stories to convey their community's cultural and natural history. *Stories from Where We Live* reinvigorates that tradition in hopes of helping young people better understand the place where they live. The anthologies feature poems, stories, and essays from historical and contemporary authors, as well as from the oral traditions of each region's indigenous peoples. Together they document the geographic richness of the continent and reflect the myriad ways that people interact with and respond to the natural world. We hope that these stories kindle readers' imaginations and inspire them to explore, observe, ponder, and protect the place they call home.

Please visit www.worldashome.org for a teaching guide to this book and more information on the *Stories from Where We Live* series.

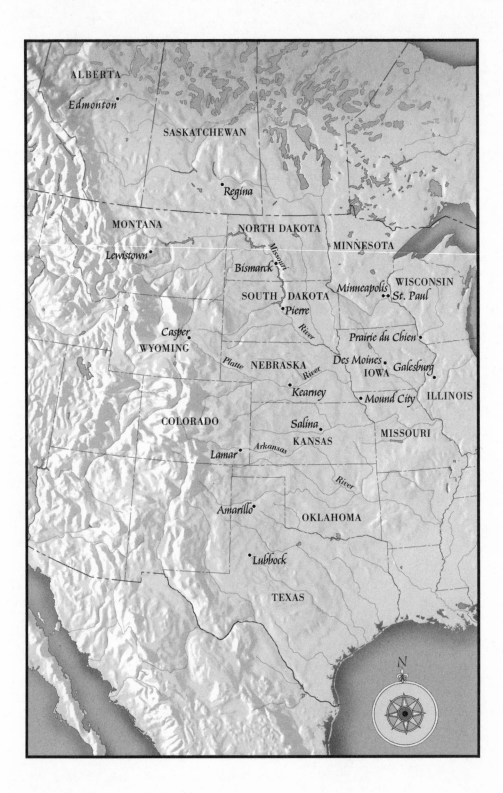

Stories from Where We Live

The Great North American Prairie

EDITED BY SARA ST. ANTOINE

Maps by Paul Mirocha
Illustrations by Trudy Nicholson

MILKWEED EDITIONS

Published 2001 by Milkweed Editions
Printed in Canada
Jacket design by Paul Mirocha
Jacket and interior illustrations by Trudy Nicholson
Jacket and interior maps by Paul Mirocha
Interior design by Wendy Holdman
The text of this book is set in Legacy.
01 02 03 04 05   5 4 3 2 1
First Edition

Milkweed Editions, a nonprofit publisher, gratefully acknowledges support from our World As
Home funders, the Lila Wallace-Reader's Digest Fund and Reader's Legacy underwriter Elly
Sturgis. Other support has been provided by the Elmer L. and Eleanor J. Andersen Foundation;
Bush Foundation; General Mills Foundation; McKnight Foundation; Minnesota State Arts
Board through an appropriation by the Minnesota State Legislature; Norwest Foundation on
behalf of Norwest Bank Minnesota; Lawrence and Elizabeth Ann O'Shaughnessy Charitable
Income Trust in honor of Lawrence M. O'Shaughnessy; Oswald Family Foundation; Ritz
Foundation on behalf of Mr. and Mrs. E. J. Phelps Jr.; John and Beverly Rollwagen Fund of the
Minneapolis Foundation; St. Paul Companies, Inc.; Target Foundation on behalf of Dayton's,
Mervyn's California and Target Stores; U.S. Bancorp; and generous individuals.

Library of Congress Cataloging-in-Publication Data

Stories from where we live—The great North American prairie / edited by Sara St. Antoine.—
1st ed.
     p.   cm. — (Stories from where we live)
Includes bibliographical references.
ISBN 1-57131-630-2 (acid-free paper)
    1. Great Plains—History—Miscellanea—Juvenile literature. 2. Prairies—United
States—Miscellanea—Juvenile literature. 3. Prairies—Canada—Miscellanea—Juvenile
literature. 4. Great Plains—Biography—Miscellanea—Juvenile literature. 5. Natural
history—Great Plains—Miscellanea—Juvenile literature. 6. Great Plains—Literary
collections. 7. American literature—Great Plains.   [1. Great Plains—Literary
collections.] I. St. Antoine, Sara, 1966–   II. Series.

F591.G75 2001
978—dc21

00-067886

Stories from Where We Live
The Great North American Prairie

Great Places

Reapers and Sowers

Wild Lives

Appendixes: Ecology of the Great North American Prairie

An Invitation

If you have ever been lucky enough to stand in the middle of a tallgrass prairie—big bluestem and blazing stars looming overhead—you may have felt for a moment the wonder of someone traveling through these grasslands two hundred years ago.

If you have ever seen the rounded curves of buffalo wallows in a prairie preserve, you may have imagined for a moment that the buffalo were right before you, rolling their great shaggy bodies in the earth.

If you have ever heard family stories about the prairie, you may look at today's communities with a greater appreciation for what they have been, and what they yet could be.

The stories of the Great North American Prairie are all around us—in our lore, in letters and journals, in the very contours of the land. We've gathered some of those stories in this book to celebrate prairie life from the past to the present day.

Our Great North American Prairie ecoregion stretches from the foothills of the Rockies to Illinois and from central Canada to west Texas. Wind and grass and sky have always been the defining elements of this vast region. But the landscape is also remarkably varied. West to east, the prairie changes from short grass to mixed grass to tall grass. Badland rocks, tall buttes, bluffs, and gullies add height and depth to the level plain. Farms and ranches cover much of the region, but here and there lie bustling cities, including Minneapolis, Des Moines, and Wichita.

Dip into the stories, poems, essays, and letters in this anthology and you'll discover some of the richness of this prairie landscape and its inhabitants. You'll hear the whistle of prairie dogs. You'll witness the dance of sandhill cranes. You'll notice the white flash of a pronghorn's tail and the yellow and black spots on a salamander's back. You'll also meet some of the diverse people who have lived in this region over the centuries.

As you'll see, the anthology is divided into four parts: "Adventures" recounts moments of drama and exploration on the prairie; "Great Places" describes tallgrass preserves, marshes, sloughs, and other favorite prairie places; "Reapers and Sowers" conveys the ways people have harvested or tended this great grassy land; and "Wild Lives" brings you up close and personal with coyotes, burrowing owls, meadowlarks, and other prairie dwellers.

We hope you enjoy these assembled prairie writings. And we hope you'll venture out into this ecoregion and create some prairie stories of your own.

—Sara St. Antoine

Stories from Where We Live

The Great North American Prairie

Adventures

The Blizzard

GARY PENLEY

Gary Penley spent his boyhood living with his mother, brother, and grand-father on a remote cattle ranch on the prairie of eastern Colorado. He de-scribes his early adventures there in his memoir, Rivers of Wind, *from which this story is drawn.*

I woke that morning in 1953 to a deadly howl. A terrific bliz-zard had hit in the night. Blizzards were our worst fear on the Colorado High Plains, and to a boy that howl was an ominous sound.

Our old rock house, built by a homesteader in the late 1800s, sat stark and alone on the prairie, miles from the near-est neighbor. Outside the windows the world appeared pure white, a swirling, violent white. The freezing wind came from the north at fifty to sixty miles per hour as snow and ice pounded the sides of the house. The temperature stood at twenty-five below zero.

Mom was already up, staring nervously out the windows at the storm. She was a strong lady and accustomed to harsh weather, but she never stopped worrying over us when we had to go out to tend the livestock.

I knew it was the worst storm I had ever seen. Dad walked

out of his room looking grim and said it was the worst he'd seen as well.

"Dad" was Mom's father, my grandfather, a flinty, snowy-haired man named George Blizzard. He had raised me from the age of two and so had become my Dad as well. His stocky, muscular body reflected a life of hard physical labor.

Dad was an intense, driven man. Armed with only a third-grade education, he had pursued a lifelong dream of owning a cattle ranch. Many things stood in the way of his dream: raising a family through hard times, the Great Depression, and World War II. At the age of sixty, however, Dad bought his first two cows and started building a ranch. A study in determination and endurance, he now spent his old age working to pay for his hard-won dream.

I stared out the window at the blizzard's fury and listened to its deadly howl. I knew we had to go out there. A rancher's fortune and responsibility lie in the cattle herd, and they couldn't survive a storm like this without shelter. We had to see if the herd had made it to the old barn and sheds one mile south of the house, the site of an abandoned homestead. Four horses were there as well, two saddle horses and two work-horses. They were all locked inside the barn, however, and reasonably safe.

Dad was an old master at driving workhorses, having done it for a living much of his life. The team he kept at the old homestead were Belgians, huge draft animals that weighed two thousand pounds each. He still worked them often.

The blizzard howled and moaned around the corners of the house as we dressed to go out. We already had on long johns and several pairs of socks. Mom helped us into heavy sweaters, coats, boots, and gloves, and admonished us to be careful. Dad put on his lined leather gloves and the heaviest wrap he owned, a long sheepskin-lined leather coat that reached to his knees, but on his head he wore his hat, his old Stetson. Regardless of the weather, he always wore that old hat.

Dad moved with purpose, his gray eyes grim and determined. I tried to be brave. We said good-bye to Mom, opened the back door to a blast of howling wind, and pushed out into the blizzard.

Dad was seventy-eight years old that morning. I was twelve.

The raw wind of a blizzard, filled with shards of ice and snow, cuts your face like a knife and sears your eyes when you try to open them. When visibility nears zero a blizzard becomes a whiteout. In a whiteout the blowing snow and ice completely fill the air; you can't tell the ground from the sky. Everything looks the same—white.

The wind greatly increases the effects of the cold. The harder it blows, the more heat it pulls from your body. Wind creates the chill factor that weathermen quote along with the actual temperature. The chill factor is what your body feels. The chill factor is what freezes you.

The high wind in a blizzard generates an extreme chill factor if the actual temperature is low. A temperature of twenty-five below with a wind of fifty to sixty miles per hour creates a chill factor greater than seventy below zero. Seventy below is what we felt that morning, and it's what we would face in the hours to come.

We leaned hard into the storm, forcing our way across the yard. The icy wind cut my face, and the cold pierced my clothes. This was too severe, colder than I'd ever felt. We didn't even own the proper clothing for these conditions.

The pickup was parked in the barn. We were already cold by the time we reached it, but it felt good to get in out of the wind. I was glad it was a strong, four-wheel drive. The big engine cranked over hard in the cold air, but after a few anxious moments it started with a roar. I began to feel more secure as the truck idled and the heater warmed the inside of the cab.

Going south the one-mile trip would be with the wind, but coming back we would face directly into it. Visibility would be a real problem; this one was truly a whiteout.

The storm's fury rocked the truck as we backed out of the barn and found our way to the road. The four-wheel drive cut through the snow smoothly, but the poor visibility forced us to move along at a crawl. Even driving with the wind we could barely make out the snow-covered ground and the narrow two-track road ahead. Several times we had to stop and sit for a few minutes to keep from losing sight of the road.

Blizzards are loud. The howling wind and ice particles beat a frightening din against the metal cab as we inched along.

The trip to the old homestead took about forty-five minutes, but we made it. The fenced-in lane that ran beside the barns and corrals provided a welcome windbreak as we drove in. It shut out some of the noise and improved the visibility. The wind still reached us in the lane, and the snow still blew, but the relative calm would help the chill factor a bit. The cold wouldn't bite quite so badly when we got out to feed the stock.

The cattle were all there, huddled up under the sheds, safe. Now we just needed to quickly feed them and the horses and then get back to the house.

We opened the pickup doors and started to step out. Suddenly the engine began to sputter, then died. We looked at each other silently and sat back down in the cab. Dad tried to start the engine. It turned over, but it wouldn't start. We knew we had plenty of gas, and we knew the battery was strong, so we sat for a few minutes and tried it again.

The engine would crank over, but it wouldn't fire. We got out and looked under the hood. Neither of us had much mechanical knowledge, but at least nothing looked wrong. There were no loose wires in sight, and no parts missing.

The cold began to penetrate quickly. We got back into the cab and tried once more to start it. Nothing.

We both knew what that meant. We couldn't survive long without the heater, and we'd already used up twenty or thirty minutes trying to get it started.

Dad sat grimly silent as our breath blew steam inside the cab. He gazed out the windshield into the storm, thinking, his face a picture of determination. Then he turned to me and said, "We can't stay here. We got matches, but the old house here has got no stove in it now, and we've got nothin' to burn anyway."

"Can't we burn the barn or something?" I asked him. "Or just tear some wood off of it and burn that?"

"Yeah, we could," he replied, "and that might work. And then again it might not. We might end up freezin' anyway.

"And there's somethin' else to think about," he said. "Your mother. She'll come after us, ya know, no matter what. If we don't make it back this mornin' she'll take off on foot if she has to, and she can't make it in this."

He was right. Mom wouldn't know what had happened to us, and even if we did save ourselves by burning the barn she'd come looking for us, and she'd have to do it on foot. She couldn't survive that, but we knew she would try.

Our minds were on the four horses in the barn; we both

knew them well. The two saddle horses were fine mounts, but they couldn't handle a storm like this. One of the workhorses, Prince, was powerful, but he didn't have the stamina. Dad looked at me and said, "You wait here. I'm goin' to get Jigs."

Jigs was a huge sorrel. He could pull out a pickup that had sunk to its axles in the mud, muscles standing out like thick ropes as he squatted his powerful hindquarters and drove his body forward on pile-driving legs, a juggernaut who didn't know the meaning of giving up. And though he possessed that tremendous spirit, Jigs was gentle as a house pet. Practically from the time I learned to walk he had let me swing on his neck, stand up and ride on his back without even a bridle on, or do any other outrageous thing I wanted. Now we were asking him to save our lives.

I waited in the cab while Dad went to the barn to harness Jigs and hitch him to the big sled. He had built the sled for feeding the cattle in deep snow. It was low and flat with no sides, simply a floor made of planks resting on stout wooden runners. The floor of the sled was about eight feet long by five feet wide and sat only one foot off the ground. Dad had to stand up on it to drive the horse. As the temperature in the cab dropped I knew Dad was even colder outside. I felt like I was freezing while I waited for him to return with Jigs.

They appeared through the blowing snow, first as a ghost-like outline, then taking shape as they drew near. Dad was standing up on the sled, and, incredibly, Jigs was holding his head high and prancing through the snow as if he were leading a parade.

They pulled up beside the pickup, and Dad hollered, "Whoa!" Jigs the giant horse looked marvelous. He was our only chance. But as much as I respected Jigs, I still had grave doubts that we could make it. I knew horses pretty well, and I knew they were extremely reluctant to leave the security of their own barn under bad conditions.

It was likely that Jigs wouldn't leave the safety of the buildings, that he would simply refuse to go into the blizzard. If he refused, we were finished. And even if he didn't, both he and Dad would have to face directly into that awful wind and endure it all the way.

I knew Dad could do it. I didn't know if Jigs could.

Dad had found an old tattered blanket somewhere and brought it for me. He sat me down on the sled, facing the rear with my back to the wind, and wrapped the blanket around me. I crossed my legs and sat on one end of the blanket to hold it down; Dad wrapped up the rest completely around my head and told me to hang on to it tightly.

Then Dad stepped up onto the sled directly behind me, picked up the reins, snapped them at Jigs, and hollered, "Hee-yah!" Jigs leaned into the harness traces and started the sled smoothly down the lane. Within a minute I felt us take a slight turn to the right as we passed out through the open gate at the end of the lane. A few more yards and we'd leave the windbreaks and head directly into the blizzard. We'd soon find out if Jigs would face it or turn back and refuse.

The blizzard roared into us, threatening to tear us from the sled. Shrieking and howling like the deadly beast that it was, it engulfed us, isolating us in its frozen violence. The wind howled around Jigs's body, around Dad's body, my body, and around the sled. It tried to tear my blanket from me, but I clung to it desperately.

Jigs was incredible. When the full force of the blizzard slammed him in the face he just lowered his head and bore into it with everything he had.

I couldn't see from under the blanket, but the snow and ice pounded me and the wind rocked me and tried to sweep me off the sled. I could hear under there, though; God, could I hear! Close by, a cracking sound, the sled runners breaking through the hard crust of the snow. And the wind, that God-awful wind, howling around us, screaming in our ears. And always Dad's voice, yelling above the wind, "Hyo! Hyo!" driving Jigs on.

When I did peek out from under the blanket I couldn't see a thing, just a swirling white mass. How could we possibly make it through this? We had to follow that little two-track road, and it was filled with snow. How could Dad and Jigs keep sight of the road in a whiteout, with that icy wind cutting their eyes all the way?

I worried that Jigs might try to make a slow turn to keep from facing the wind directly. If they lost the road for only a moment, we'd wander off onto the prairie and be lost. We probably wouldn't last more than an hour after that.

I looked out and around toward Dad once, into the wind. I could just make out his outline—that stout old frame, standing like a rock, leaning hard into the wind and yelling, ever yelling to Jigs.

I wondered how Dad and Jigs could stand to face that cold. I still do.

Jigs faltered several times and nearly went down. Each time he stumbled Dad hollered even louder. Jigs picked up the pace again each time and fought on.

In my terror I'd forgotten all about the cold. Suddenly it came back to me. My body was freezing, and my hands and feet felt numb. I couldn't move my fingers. My hands simply felt like weights at the ends of my arms, and my feet were nearly as bad. I was beginning to freeze.

Jigs fell. He stumbled, staggered, and went down. Thrashing and pawing in the harness traces, he jerked the sled in spasms. Bawling and blowing in terror, he pawed frantically to regain his feet. Dad's steady voice became soothing, cajoling, encouraging. "Come on, Jigs. Come on, boy. You can do it."

Then with an effort beyond belief, Jigs heaved himself to his feet, drew a long, rasping breath, lowered his head, and struggled on. To his eternal credit, Jigs never once tried to turn away from the freezing wind. He faced it all the way. And so did Dad.

I rode that sled backward forever, listening, fearing, praying. We had to be lost. We'd been traveling too long. We should have been there by now. We could be anywhere. We probably wouldn't even know where we were when the end came, when we became just a snow-covered hump on the prairie.

The sled dipped in front, went down a slight grade and back up the other side. Something felt familiar. Then I knew. It felt like the draw, only a couple of hundred yards from the house. Was that possible? A minute later Dad hollered, "Whoa," and we stopped.

I peered out from under my blanket. I could just make out the corral fence through the blowing snow. The corral fence. We had made it.

I stood up stiffly, stepped off the sled, and walked to the front. Dad stood by Jigs, holding the reins, his tired arms hanging at his sides. The most heroic pair I've ever seen, they were an awesome sight.

Jigs looked like a giant ice sculpture. Long icicles hung from his mane, and thousands of smaller ones hung from his hair, covering his entire body. His lower legs were pillars of packed snow and ice. His face was completely frozen over, and both his eyes and his nostrils had nearly frozen shut. His heavy breath forced puffs of steam from two small holes in the ice that covered his nose.

I don't know how Jigs lived through it, but as spent as he was, when I touched his shoulder he raised his head and stood tall and proud, as if he knew he'd just done something great. He was magnificent.

And Dad. He looked like he wasn't alive. The front of his great sheepskin coat and the legs of his Levi's were a solid sheet of ice, a quarter of an inch thick. His old hat looked like it was made of ice. Icicles hung from his eyebrows, down over his eyes, and his face had been beaten bright red by the wind. But there he stood. He'd faced that blizzard all the way, just like I'd known he would. His eyes were pained now, but still grim. A spark of defiance gleamed in those eyes too, a spark that said, "By God, we did it."

Dad pointed to the house and motioned for me to go in, then motioned that he was going to put Jigs in the barn. I couldn't talk, but I hugged that great horse's neck before I left them.

I trudged to the house, so frozen I could barely walk. Mom opened the door and gasped, "Gary, what happened?"

I couldn't answer. I could only shake my head.

"Where's Dad?" she asked frantically. I pointed back toward the barn.

"Is he all right?"

I nodded that he was.

She took off my cap, slowly pulled off my gloves, and looked at my hands. Then she rubbed them gently and asked, "Can you feel that?"

I shook my head. I couldn't feel a thing. Mom looked as if she might cry, but she didn't. She pulled off my coat, poured some cool water in the wash pan, and told me to put my hands in it. I couldn't feel anything at first, but in a few minutes they began to thaw, and with that came the pain. As the pain of my hands thawing became nearly unbearable I began to cry, and with that I began to talk. Mom stood in horror as I told her what had happened to us.

We waited a long time for Dad to come in. It seemed to be taking too long just to put Jigs in the barn. At last he limped through the door, barely able to stand. He had put Jigs in the barn before he came in, taken off his harness, and fed him. He couldn't talk either, but he mumbled something about Jigs having earned a good meal.

I'm sure Dad did something else before he came to the house that morning. I know he petted old Jigs, and thanked him for saving our lives.

More than forty years have passed since that blizzard, yet some memory of it still returns to me nearly every day. In my mind it's often the scene of Jigs prancing through the blowing snow when he and Dad first appeared with the sled, or the two of them covered with ice at the end. I still hear the sounds, too—the awful howling of the wind, and Dad's voice, yelling above the storm, driving Jigs on.

***

Gary Penley *is the author of* Rivers of Wind: A Western Boyhood Remembered *(Filter Press). The book won first place in the Colorado Book Publishers Awards in 1998.*

Outside Abilene

HARLEY ELLIOTT

the full rage of kansas
turns loose upon us.

On the Mexican radio station
they are singing *Espiritu de mis sueños*
and that is
exactly it tonight.

The spirit of my dreams
rises in the storm like vapor.

Deep clouds bulge together
and below them
we are a tiny constellation of lights
the car
laid under sheets of lightning
moving straight in to the night.

Before us are miles
and miles of water and wind.

Harley Elliott *is a poet and visual artist living in Salina, Kansas. His poetry has been published in more than two hundred small-press magazines and in nine of his own books. He is a lifelong resident of the prairie, and it continues to inform his work.*

Homestead Girl

CINDY ROGERS

Early prairie homesteaders left the security of their towns, friends, and families to start their new lives in the West. This story is based on some of the true stories that Cindy Rogers's grandparents told her about their years on the Dakota frontier.

The first time I heard Papa mention the advertisement, I was sitting at the table shelling a mess of garden peas.

"It's free land," Papa says, "if we go west and claim it."

Mama is filling a bowl with fresh-cut purple-and-yellow pansies. "There must be a hitch," she says.

Papa shakes his head, takes out his pocketknife, and cuts the notice from the newspaper. "Nope. We homestead it. The advertisement says to build a house, dig a well, and plant a crop. Then, if we live there five years, the land is ours."

I roll Whiskers's ball of string under the table with my foot and watch him flick his gray tail back and forth, then pounce. "Where is the West, Papa?"

Papa strokes his mustache as he calculates. "I figure it's seven days on the other side of the Mississippi, Jessie Sarah. Several days by train."

That's a long way. Why would Papa be excited about a place so far away? For some reason, I feel relieved when my friend

Lillian comes by to play. We skip out the door and across the lane to the woods, away from Papa's words. But every day when Papa comes home from the livery stable where he works, he and Mama talk about the advertisement.

"Maude, imagine owning so much land."

Mama nods as she helps me tie my row of hollyhocks to the front porch. "Plenty of space for a big garden and a flock of chickens. I wonder if there are mountains."

They never ask what I think, but I can tell that Mama is catching Papa's fever. I grab Whiskers and we climb high, high into the big oak tree. Up there I can't hear any talk about homesteading.

One hot summer day, Papa loads up the lumber wagon with lots of supplies: jars of Grandmama's beets and pickles, a big bag of flour, feed sacks for the horses, a kettle, and a tin pan. He kisses Mama and me good-bye.

"Don't go, Papa," I beg.

"I must see this land for myself," he says. "Help your Mama, homestead girl." He climbs aboard and heads the horses down the lane.

"I'm not a homestead girl!" I yell as the creaking wagon disappears.

The first week I learn to milk Bessie by myself. And I go to the mailbox every day. By the second week, I can harness Morgan to the buggy almost as fast as Mama.

"I wonder if Papa is lost in the West," I say at the third Sunday dinner with Granddad and Grandmama.

"Don't worry, Jessie Sarah," says Mama. "We'll hear from him soon." Still, worry lines cross her forehead.

A letter finally arrives. I wish it hadn't.

Pack up. Come west. It says more, but I stop listening.

"It will be a grand adventure," Mama says over and over, jutting out her chin.

But the day she sells our house with its white fence and climbing morning glory, her chin quivers. "You'll need to trim that honeysuckle vine every year," she says to Mr. Halvorson. She clears her throat and gazes at the house. "I'll leave the lace curtain in the kitchen. It will be a welcome for your wife."

My friend Lillian gathers up pine needles, flower petals, acorns, and seeds from our front yard and makes a sweet-smelling sachet. "Take this with you, Jessie Sarah," she says, her eyes big and bright. "Remember me and Wisconsin every time you smell it." I push it deep into my dress pocket.

One last time Whiskers and I climb the oak tree. One more time I check the ties on my hollyhocks. One final time I play in the woods with Lillian.

The train is very long. Mama and I aren't the only ones moving west. Granddad helps us load Morgan, Bessie, a crate of baby chicks, and all our belongings into a railroad boxcar. "Here's a shovel, Jessie Sarah. You'll need it, dear girl."

I hold on to him extra tight when I say good-bye. Mama cries, too. One more time I wait for her to change her mind. But she blows her nose into Granddad's handkerchief, juts out her chin, and climbs aboard.

I help Mama make a home in the corner of the boxcar. I make hiding places for Whiskers among the kerosene jugs, the barrels of pots and books, the burlap feed and seed sacks. I dangle my legs over the handles of Papa's new hand plow. We eat our meals on top of the crate of Haviland china. I keep Lillian's sachet close to my nose when we rest under Grandmama's best quilt.

I make speeches about homesteading on top of the cook

stove: "LAND. FREE LAND. WIDE-OPEN SPACES. MOVE WEST." I decide I don't like speechmaking and act out fairy tales in the washtub instead.

Even on a train, Bessie needs milking. I tell Whiskers he can have all the fresh milk he wants, but still that cat keeps a sly eye on Mama's crate of peeping baby chicks.

"Jessie Sarah, look!" says Mama one morning at the boxcar door.

I stare down, down through the stone arches of the railroad bridge. My voice sounds as shaky as Grandmama's when we left her behind. "Is it the Mississippi?"

Mama nods. "We've crossed to the West."

And just like the moving river, I know, at last, that there is no turning back.

The train stops several times a day, but by the third day I can't shovel away all the smells. Morgan stomps his hooves. "I know how you feel," I tell him. "I want to be out running, too."

At last we arrive in western Dakota. Although the train wheels no longer move beneath our feet, a strong wind pushes

us toward the acres and acres of prairie grasses.

"We're being dropped in the middle of nowhere," says Mama, grabbing her sunbonnet, her face as pale as the butter she's been churning.

The sky is immense, and I feel as small as a flea on Morgan's broad back. I see more blue than I've ever seen at one time in my life. I can see from one horizon to the other without a tree or building or town breaking the view.

But the prairie is not completely empty, for there, coming across the prairie in his lumber wagon, is Papa, a big smile plastered across his tanned face. He looks taller and thinner somehow, and when he jumps from his wagon, his strides toward us are long and strong. He swoops Mama and me up in the kind of hug that doesn't let go.

"I thought maybe, at the last minute, you wouldn't be able to leave," he whispers in our ears.

Despite Papa's warm arms, I look around the empty train stop and the windy treeless prairie and decide that maybe the hardest part won't have been in the leaving, but in the staying.

Papa ties Bessie to the back of the wagon and grins at me. "You've grown over the summer, homestead girl. Are you ready to go home?"

Home? My heart flutters. Oh, but he means this home. This homestead land. "I . . . I don't see any climbing trees. And Papa, I don't know how to be a homestead girl."

He smiles. "You can help me break the sod," he says, harnessing Morgan with his other horses.

I wonder if breaking the sod is like breaking the wildness out of a horse, like breaking the homesickness out of me.

We load the wagon, tying everything down as best we can. I try to leave the jug of cod-liver oil behind. "Go fetch it, Jessie Sarah," says Mama, tying her bonnet firmly under her chin. "It will keep us from getting sick in this barren country."

We travel across the wide plains most of the day, the wagon wheels and horses kicking up clouds of dust. The wind grabs most of it, twirling it into a long trail of gray behind us. Giant pillow clouds, piled one on top of the other, try to fill the endless sky. Prairie grasses so tall I can't always see above them swoosh like the waves on Lake Wisconsin.

"Can you smell the sage?" Papa asks. He calls out the names of the wildflowers. "Asters, goatsbeard, wild prairie rose, snakeweed, buffalo bur."

The coneflowers with their dancing yellow skirts are my favorite. In my pocket I feel Lillian's nubby sachet. I will make one of Dakota's wildflowers for her.

Here and there, huge tabletop hills squat above the rolling land. "Those are buttes," says Papa. "Rainy Butte . . . Grassy Butte . . . Black Butte." Then he whispers, "See the antelope up ahead? They look like deer, don't they?" I count eleven of the pretty horned animals before they bound away, their fluffy white backsides bouncing above the grass like popcorn in a pan.

At long last Papa stops the wagon. "There," he says, pointing. "There's our homestead claim."

The wind has died down. The round orange sun is settling close to the horizon, its persimmon-colored sunset stretching far in both directions. I spot a small shed.

Mama shades her eyes. "Where's the house, Joe?"

Papa strokes his mustache and says really fast, "For right now, it's just a one-room shack, Maude. There's not enough lumber out in these parts yet. But next summer we'll build a real frame house." Mama stares at the mound of sod and tar paper.

"But Papa," I say, "what will I do for a climbing tree?" There haven't been any trees all day. I guess I'm just hoping.

A prairie dog yips and jerks its tail up and down like a pump handle. Whiskers snaps his tail back and forth, then leaps out of the wagon box.

The shed is cool inside, but it feels like a playhouse. We'll have to sit on the beds to eat at the table. I think Papa forgot to build a floor.

While I trail along behind, Papa walks Mama across the dusk-touched claim. "I see a field of wheat over there and oats here." Papa's arm moves in great arcs. "And right here I see the barn and your garden. I planted some potatoes and corn between that rise and the house." He sounds excited, as if he'd already built and planted it all.

I look across the darkening land where nothing is tall enough to cast a shadow. "Will we plant oak trees, too? And are there other homesteaders out here?"

Papa swoops me up in a waltzlike hug. "We can try, Jessie Sarah. And yes, homesteaders are arriving every week." He twirls me around, grabbing Mama's hand as he goes. "Soon we will have neighbors there . . . and there . . . and there." Then, with a final sweep of his arm, he says, "The whole of the house shall have a porch. We will swing and gaze ten miles in every direction. You will need bushels of hollyhocks and morning glory to cover its length."

As I stand beside Papa I try to see it all just as he says. But . . . whatever will I do without Lillian? And Granddad and Grandmama? And a climbing tree?

Mama eyes the distant shape that appears no bigger than an outhouse. "Enough dreaming," she says. "We best get to unpacking." She hesitates, then picks up her skirt and marches through the rutted prairie toward the wagon.

Like Mama, I jut out my chin . . . and then I see it, as if for the first time. Beyond the sod hut, rising at great sharp angles, stands a butte. Black Butte. It looks much bigger, stretches far higher, and seems to promise more adventure than the tallest tree in Wisconsin.

I shiver just thinking about it. Suddenly I feel better, almost happy. Maybe there will be new neighbors, soon, like

Papa says. And maybe Granddad and Grandmama will come for a visit and decide to stay, like Mama says.

"Let's go, homestead girl," calls Papa.

I hop over a thistle weed, then run across our big wide land to grab his callused hand. Maybe I can be a homestead girl, after all.

Cindy Rogers *is a native North Dakotan, now living in Minnesota. The prairie setting often plays a role in the stories and articles she writes for children's and family publications.*

Midway Morning

ROBIN E. KELSEY

The farm belt meets the big city in the rail yards of Minneapolis and St. Paul. These industrial areas can be surprisingly attractive to city folks in search of solitude and wide-open spaces.

When I was twelve, Saturday morning was the time I liked best. One Saturday in May, I got up while the light was still pale, put on a pair of jeans, a sweatshirt, and a baseball jacket, and left the house by the kitchen door. The squirrels were scrabbling and fussing high in the elm tree, and somewhere nearby a mourning dove lamented another day. The rest of the world was tucked away, asleep. Even the long grass of the back-yard slumped under the dew.

Grabbing my bike, I set off down the alley, past Rita Berg's house, the MacAllisters' garden, and the house on the corner, whose owner I didn't know. I stood on the pedals and leaned forward, pressing my body into the wind. The chilly air invigorated me, and my freedom did, too. Kids who hit me at school and people who didn't listen were nowhere to be seen.

When I reached the end of the block, I turned left, away from the park. The old meadow with its rabbits and snakes was long gone, torn up and covered with bright green sod and a new athletic field. The park planners had put in winding asphalt bike paths, but riding them was tedious, like running on a track. And besides, people might be walking their dogs there this early in the morning, and I wasn't ready for company.

Instead I headed east along the frontage road, past the old brick warehouses with their broken windows and faded yellow doors. I made a slalom of the wide road, my rubber tires grinding sand against the concrete, and the chrome of my fender glinting in the first rays of the sun. The world grew big in this deserted place. Far off, trains in the switching yard coupled and uncoupled with a dull clang and a strain of diesel engines.

I could see my destination in the distance. Past the warehouses, towering above the flat plain of the city, stood a grain elevator. Two rows of white cylinders—silos full of corn, wheat, and soybeans—rose up many stories tall. Attached to the rows of cylinders was a boxy building, even taller, with a peaked roof sheltering tiny windows that looked out over the city.

The silos made me think of my parents' friends, the Abrahamsons, and their family farm out by Mud Lake, north of Willmar. Old Ned Abrahamson still worked the farm even though he was almost eighty. Like farmers all over southern Minnesota and the Dakotas, Ned shipped his grain to the Twin Cities, where it was stored and then shipped again to all parts of the country. The heart of this activity was the Midway, where I was headed, a great lonely space of grain elevators and freight cars between Minneapolis and St. Paul.

Another mile more and I turned right, my bike shuddering as it bumped over an abandoned set of rails. Before me loomed the scalloped wall of the elevator. To the left lay a wide stretch of beaten dirt, pocked with tufts of brown grass and abandoned pieces of equipment, giving way to the southeast to a scruffy field. I pulled up on my bike, dismounted, and leaned it against a small shed of corrugated aluminum.

Here, amidst the white silos, the morning light was especially fine, and overhead the sky, blown wide by the spaces of the Midway, stretched out its guarantee of blue. I walked along the abandoned tracks, through goldenrod and ragweed and wildflowers whose names I didn't know. Ned Abrahamson told me once that here and there along the rail beds you could find pieces of prairie tucked among the weeds. I found a discarded brown bottle, which, when I held it up in front of my eyes, made the world look like an old photograph. Strange as it may seem, I felt closer to the earth here than

at the park. Among the grain elevators, life was messy and rich. I saw hawks here, as well as rabbits, woodchucks, and a heron down by the trickling stream that ran beneath the frontage road. Today I was happy to watch sparrows picking through the stalks and stems of the rail beds, and a field mouse darting out from under a rusting bin.

During my ramble in the Midway, I daydreamed. I wondered what my life would be like if I became the starting second baseman for the Twins. I thought about waking up one day as a brilliant mathematician, able to correct the homework of my classmate Benjamin Gegler, who was already taking trigonometry. I imagined Wayne Thurmond, who tormented me relentlessly during band practices, falling into an icy lake. In my fantasies, Wayne always made it to shore, but just barely, and not before he had lost that ugly cap he always wore. But mainly my dreams dissolved into vague wishes that surface still, years later, from time to time.

When I got back on my bike and headed home, the best of the morning was gone. The air had become warm and lazy, and the occasional car zipped past on the frontage road. The squirrels had stopped their chattering. Ms. Berg was out retrieving her paper from the dry grass, and Mr. Fitzer, who lived across the street, was already putting a new coat of paint on his front porch. I parked my bike next to the push mower by the side of the house. It would be another week before I would have the world to myself again.

❧

Robin E. Kelsey *grew up in Minneapolis, Minnesota, and now lives on the East Coast. He has practiced law and studied art history. He misses the grain elevators of the Midway and visits them every so often.*

Song of the Crow and Owl

ŚIYA´KA

At night may I roam
Against the winds may I roam
At night may I roam
When the owl is hooting
May I roam.

At dawn may I roam
Against the winds may I roam
At dawn may I roam
When the crow is calling
May I roam.

Śiya´ka, *or* **Teal Duck,** *was an elected Teton Sioux chief. As a young man, he sought out a dream that would give him guidance in his life, and then had a powerful dream that featured a crow and an owl. The dream inspired this song, which he shared with ethnologist Frances Densmore in 1912.*

Corn

E. G. WILLY

A broad swath of the Great North American Prairie region is covered with cornfields, which produce more than half of all the corn grown in the United States. Small wonder, then, that rustling rows of corn figure prominently in the memories and stories of so many prairie people.

There was corn, and corn, and more corn. The prairie of western Iowa was covered with it, a vast sea of rippling stalks that whispered like snakes in the harvest wind. It was 1964. And the summer was hot. We did a lot of swimming that summer. We had a local pool, a cattle trough filled with fresh water. Although I wasn't really old enough to swim that year, and the water really wasn't deep enough in the trough, it sure made for cool times for us kids in the Midwest summer. We were pretty glad we had something to wade in, although my mother's canning partner, Mrs. Larousse, insisted that our swimming pool was going to give us all polio and we were going to end up on crutches. No one seemed to listen to her much, seeing as there was a vaccine for polio and all of us had taken it. So it was a pretty good summer. And the farmers were happy about it. And the crop looked like a good one to everyone but me.

That was the year I got lost in the corn. I don't know how I managed it. I don't think there was more than a hundred acres of corn across from our barn. And the next crop over, on Slim's farm, was separated from ours by a barbed-wire fence. But somehow I found a way to lose myself in there.

Alan Kootz, the farmer kid on the spread across from ours, sent me out there. He was a couple years older than I was, my brother's friend, a rough kid by anyone's description. "Ed, go on out there. I'll meet you on the other side," invited Alan.

"Which way?"

"Thataway." Alan pointed a dirty finger into the center of the field. Alan was always chewing on his nails, right down to the quick. The farm dirt would get trapped under his skin, blacken his fingers. "Go on. Try it out."

"I don't know."

"Go on. It's fun out there."

"What if I get lost?"

"You can't get lost in corn. It's all the same," said Alan. "Anyone knows that."

"You'll come and get me?"

"Sure I will."

At first it was okay out there in the corn. I could turn right and left and run straight ahead and always know I was in the corn. It was a pretty good feeling to be surrounded by all that rich growth. But after a while I started to get worried. As a kid you can't see over the top of the corn. It's as tall as the tallest man. And every row is identical to the row before it, the same as the row behind it. You can't see where your feet have been when the summer is hot and the ground is dry. There are no directions inside the corn, no landmarks to grab ahold of. No matter which way I walked it seemed like the corn was never ending, that it went on and on into a forest of cornstalks that went right across the prairie, right around the whole world.

If I had been a few years older, I don't think I would have panicked. But when the wind starts blowing, the corn begins to whisper. It says all kinds of things. It started saying my name first. *"Edward . . . Edward . . . Edward . . ."*

Because I didn't know who or what voices were calling me and had been told by my mother to avoid strangers, I began to run. The wind came up good then and the corn hissed, *"Faster, run faster!"*

I found the corner of the crop when I ran into the fence at Slim's property. I caught my suspenders on the wire, tore free, and crossed over into Slim's corn. The wind blew harder, and the corn began to howl, *"Git out! Git out of here!"*

When I met a second fence, I wasn't sure if it was the crop on the other side of Slim's place or ours. The wind was constant now, the corn whispering jumbles of words I couldn't make out so well. *"Salash, salash . . . how hem now, how hem now . . . distance, distance . . . pass, pass, pass . . . ver, ver, ver . . ."*

After a while, I was run out. I stopped in between a couple of rows and lay down on the soil. It wasn't so bad on the ground. I pushed my belly into the soil and held onto the cornstalks around me. I don't remember now if it was the fertilizer, the dried bits of corn, or just the earth, but everything smelled good, just like honey. And if I breathed deeply, I was almost able to forget the whispering of the corn on the wind. I rolled up into a ball, cried softly, and pressed myself into the ground.

Slim and his old bird dog, Heidi, found me a couple of hours later. I was asleep, bundled up in the row, covered in dust and corn silk, my shirt wet from crying.

"What are you doing in there, Ed?" asked Slim with a nudge of his boot.

"Huh?" I said, still sleepy.

"You lost?"

"I guess."

"Well, you either know if you're lost or you're not. Looks to me like you're lost."

"I got scared. I couldn't find my way out."

"Yeah, it seems like a whole lot of corn when you're inside it," noted Slim.

"Yeah."

"You hear the corn talking to you?"

I nodded.

"Same thing happened to me when I was a boy." Slim tousled my hair. I grinned, glad to know I wasn't the only one who heard voices in the corn. "Caught in the breadbasket."

"What?"

"Lots of life in the corn," he pointed out. "All kinds of things if you look real close, lots of flies, blackbirds, crows, pheasants, ground squirrels, sometimes even foxes. It's just a big breadbasket, calling everyone to supper. Probably called you, too."

"I suppose so."

"Come on. We'll pick a row back."

I followed Slim back to his farm. On the way he talked a lot about the corn, how everything lived off it. Slim was a sharp old guy. He had been born in another century. His ma was Sioux. His dad was a farmer. And his skin was a patch of dark wrinkles that went around him like a road map. My dad said there wasn't much that Slim didn't know, and if Slim didn't know it, he was pretty sure his dog, Heidi, did. I was sure he was right.

Slim drove me back to our farm in his Chevy pickup. Heidi was right next to me. My folks were glad to see me, although I could see my ma was pretty upset. She looked like she was as worried as I was out there in the cornfield. She started yelling when I got out of the car. My dad didn't say a thing. Then my ma offered Slim some money for finding me. And he turned it down, said it was only what a neighbor would do. I don't think my ma would've offered money at any other time, but she was so upset, she wasn't acting normal. I explained everything that happened, how I went in the corn, how the corn started whispering my name, how Slim found me out there. Things settled down after that. Everyone laughed when I said the corn was talking to me. But it was good laughter. And I was glad to be back at the house, even though I hadn't been that far away for the last few hours.

That evening Alan Kootz was hanged by his feet off the lift in his yard. His dad, Dean Kootz, invited us over to see it. He had Alan tied by the feet. And Alan was shouting and thrashing around, his face all red. He was pretty upset. My dad asked that Mr. Kootz let Alan down.

"Just teaching him a lesson," said Mr. Kootz. "You don't send little kids off in the cornfield. Alan should know better than that."

Then my dad and Mr. Kootz got in an argument. It was a quiet argument, not a whole lot of yelling, and eventually Alan was let down, although I think he would have been up there a lot less if my dad and Mr. Kootz hadn't gotten upset with each other.

Things weren't so good between us and the Kootz family after that. My brother continued to play with Alan, and I sometimes tagged along, but mostly I chose to follow Slim around. He always had a lot of interesting things to talk about—how to make a fishing hook from a twig, how to hypnotize a chicken by drawing a line in front of it in the dirt, how to catch a pheasant by soaking layer's mash—a special feed for egg hens—in beer and leaving it at the edge of the cornfield.

When the silos got filled at the end of the season, it was a big affair. Thousands of tons of corn kernels were pumped into the steel storage containers. The activity was almost too much for us to bear. We wanted to get close to watch the loading going on but kept getting shooed off by our folks. Our cattle trough, the local swimming pool, had been closed a few weeks earlier, and there wasn't much excitement around. We kids on the farm kept talking about the pool like it had never closed. We had swimming on the brain and kept scheming about how we could get us a pool to wade in.

"You know what?" announced Alan Kootz one afternoon as we sat in the barn and observed the silo loading.

"What's that?" asked my brother.

"We can still go swimming."

"Isn't it kind of cool today?" asked my brother. He was right. The summer was over, and the cool was starting to settle in the Midwest. You can always feel it coming. At first it's a barely noticeable scent in the morning, then it starts to build, the cool whooshing in from Canada in the morning, the breeze picking up across the prairie, making the fields splash like waves on the sea.

"We can swim in the corn."

"Huh?" asked my brother. "It's all harvested."

"No, in the silo."

"Slim says you can drown in the silo," I pointed out. "Says the air's bad."

"You can't drown in corn," said my brother. "You can put your head in a bucket of it and still breathe."

"Sure, and you can't sink in it either," Alan pointed out, tossing a piece of straw from the barn with his ever dirty fingers. "You can swim right on the top of it without going under."

"Slim says there's no life inside those silos," I said. "Things go in there, they don't come out alive."

"What does Slim know? He's just an old half-breed," said Alan. "He shouldn't even have that farm."

"Yeah, just an old Indian," agreed my brother. "They talk like that."

I didn't reply. Our family came out of the Black Hills in South Dakota. My grandpa loved the Indians, had even lived on the reservation. My cousins hated them. A gathering of the family often would bring heated discussions on Indians. I was surprised my brother was saying that about Slim. We never talked bad about Indians, especially in the presence of my grandpa.

"Come on, let's go take a dip," said Alan.

I followed my brother and Alan to one of the silos. It was only just starting to get filled with corn. I watched as my brother and Alan took off their clothes and started swimming in the grain. They looked like a couple of swimming fools, hooting and tossing their arms around, acting like they were swimming.

"Hey, Ed, close that door. It's getting cold in here," shouted my brother.

I closed the door. It sure was cold in there, though I wasn't sure it would get any warmer with the door closed. Alan and my brother swam back and forth, dove in the corn, surfaced, plowed through the kernels like a pair of hogs. I watched them swim, mesmerized by their simulation.

We didn't hear Slim coming, engrossed as we were in the activity. He was suddenly just right there. Alan was doing a backstroke. My brother was in the middle of a dive. My dad was standing behind Slim, looking worried.

"What are you kids doing in here?" asked Slim. The way he said it ran a chill through my bones. My brother surfaced and looked around sheepishly.

"We're swimming," said Alan.

"Get on out of there and put on your clothes," ordered Slim.

"You don't belong here, Slim," said Alan darkly. "My dad says you're Indian-spooking the corn."

Slim cleared his throat and looked away.

"Get on out, boys, and put your clothes on," said my father evenly, although I could see he was pretty upset. "Don't you know you can drown in here?"

My brother rolled to the side of the tank and started putting on his clothes.

"We're not drowning. We're swimming," said Alan.

"Get out now," said my dad.

Alan got on his knees and crawled through the corn to his clothes.

I went outside. I could tell my dad and Slim were angry, even though they were doing their best to hide it.

Alan and my brother came out a few minutes later. My

brother's face was red from crying. Alan was looking at any-thing but the ground. He'd been crying too. My dad marched them back to the farmhouse. I walked behind with Slim.

"They get spanked in there?" I asked.

"Naw, your dad couldn't spank those boys," said Slim. "Nor could I. They're not my boys."

"You yell at them?"

"We didn't say a thing," Slim replied.

"Really?"

"Let the corn do the talking," said Slim knowingly.

I nodded, figured it was my brother's turn to hear the corn. But when I asked him about it later, he got upset. "Corn don't talk, Ed. What kind of fool thinks plants can talk?"

I was about to mention what Slim had said to me, but de-cided against it. My brother didn't look too interested in hearing it, especially after getting caught like that, then cry-ing and all.

That evening I went up to the silo, pressed my ear against the cool, steel walls of the granary, checked if there were any words coming out. I thought if I listened hard enough, I'd hear the corn talking, maybe discussing what happened in there that afternoon. But the silo was empty of voices, silent as a December morning. I plunked a stone against the building, heard the hollow echo of darkness. In the distance, Slim's prize Rhode Island rooster gave a nervous holler. An owl shrieked above in the darkness.

I made my way back to the farmhouse, cut along the path where the barbed wire met the harvested cornfield. Not much remained out there but broken, flattened stalks of corn. I pressed down a strand of barbed wire, crouched, then slipped into the cornfield. A wind was blowing across the prairie. It flicked the corn dust into the air, stirred the night, rattled the branches in the trees along the windbreak. I turned into the rushing wind and listened as it brought messages of the coming winter.

⌣

E. G. Willy, *a native of Iowa, is a resident of the San Francisco Bay Area. He writes magazine articles, radio pieces, fiction, poetry, and cartoons; is a partner in the Hot House Group, a film-production company; and is the cofounder of Ultimate Habitats, an adventure-travel company that explores the wildest forests and rivers of Latin America.*

Mollie Goodnight

ELAINE TERRANOVA

Mollie Goodnight often accompanied her husband, Charles, on cattle drives along the Goodnight-Loving Trail. This cattle trail ran from west Texas to Wyoming and was forged by Charles Goodnight and Oliver Loving after the Civil War.

On the trail my task
is to catch the change
of horses morning and afternoon.
Left to myself, I seek out
wild plum for pie. At dusk
the cattle pool before us,
dropping singly out of the hills
like sluggish streams. Then
the dark comes in, leaving
no room for anything else.

In storms on darkest nights
the cows call out to us
like babies. I sit it out
with them, no longer thinking of
what crawls here, what stings.
All I am afraid of is my own

small nature, the soft flesh
that lightens my bones, a fondness
for silk, music, a touch.

At dawn we watch the weather
lifting off the hills
for higher country. It is never
silent here. There is such
commotion, the creaking grass, wind
from the great distant mountain.

Elaine Terranova *is the author of two books of poems,* The Cult of the Right Hand, *winner of the Walt Whitman Award, and* Damages. *She has done a verse translation of Euripides'* Iphigenia at Aulis, *published in the Penn Greek Drama Series.*

Riding the Rails

CARL SANDBURG

During the late 1800s and early 1900s, thousands of men traveled the country as hoboes, hopping trains in search of food, work, and adventure. Poet Carl Sandburg began his hobo journey from his hometown of Galesburg, Illinois, one of the largest rail yards in the Midwest.

I was nineteen years old, nearly a grown man. And I was restless. The jobs I'd had all seemed dead-end with no future that called to me. Among the boys I could hold my own. With the girls I was bashful and couldn't think of what to say till after I left them, and then I wasn't sure. I had never found a "steady." . . .

What came over me in those years 1896 and 1897 wouldn't be easy to tell. I hated my home town and yet I loved it. And I hated and loved myself about the same as I did the town and the people. I came to see that my trouble was inside of myself more than it was in the town and the people.

I decided in June of 1897 to head west and work in the Kansas wheat harvest. I would beat my way on the railroads; I would be a hobo and a "gaycat." I had talked with hoboes enough to know there is the professional tramp who never works and the gaycat who hunts work and hopes to go on and get a job that suits him. I would take my chances on breaking away from my home town where I knew every street and people in every block and farmers on every edge of town.

I had never been very far from Galesburg. I was sixteen when for the first time I rode a railroad train for fifty miles. I opened a little bank of dimes and found I had eighty cents. My father got me a pass on the Q. and I rode alone to Peoria and felt important and independent. I saw the State Fair and sat a long time looking at the Illinois River and the steamboats. I was a traveler seeing the world, and when I got home I couldn't help telling other people how Peoria looked to me. . . .

Now I would take to The Road. The family didn't like the idea. Papa scowled. Mama kissed me and her eyes had tears after dinner one noon when I walked out of the house with my hands free, no bag or bundle, wearing a black-sateen shirt, coat, vest, and pants, a slouch hat, good shoes and socks, no underwear. In my pockets were a small bar of soap, a razor, a comb, a pocket mirror, two handkerchiefs, a piece of string, needles and thread, a Waterbury watch, a knife, a pipe and a sack of tobacco, three dollars and twenty-five cents.

It was the last week in June, an afternoon bright and cool. A little west of the Santa Fe station stood a freight train waiting for orders. As the train started I ran along and jumped into a boxcar. I stood at the open side door and watched the running miles of young corn. Crossing the long bridge over the Mississippi my eyes swept over it with a sharp hunger that the grand old river satisfied. Except for my father, when riding to Kansas to buy land, no one of our family had seen the Father of Waters. As the train slowed down in Fort Madison, I jumped out.

I bought a nickel's worth of cheese and crackers and sat

eating and looking across the Mississippi. The captain of a small steamboat said I could work passage to Keokuk unloading kegs of nails. I slept on the boat, had breakfast, sailed down the river watching fields and towns go by—at Burlington, Quincy, Keokuk shouldering kegs of nails to the wharves. At Keokuk I spread newspaper on green grass near a canal and slept in the open. I washed my face and hands at the canal, using soap from my pocket and drying with a handkerchief. Then I met a fellow who said, "On the road?" When I said "Yes," he led me to where he had been eating bread and meat unwrapped from a newspaper. "I got three lumps last night," he said, and handed me a lump. A lump was what you were handed if you got something to eat at a house where you asked for it. My new friend said, "I got a sitdown before I got the lumps." At one house he had been asked to sit at the kitchen table and eat. Then because he wanted to have this day free to look at the canal and the blue sky, he went from house to house for lumps, hiding them under wooden sidewalks so his hands were empty. The lump he gave me had four slices of buttered bread and two thick cuts of roast beef. "This is breakfast and dinner for me," I said.

His face and hands were pudgy as though your fingers would sink into them if you touched them. He had come out of a Brooklyn orphan asylum, had taken to The Road, and said he had never done a day's work in his life. He was proud he had found a way to live without working. He named Cincinnati Slim and Chicago Red and other professional tramps he had traveled with, as though they were big names known to all tramps and I must have heard of them. He named towns where jail food was good and how in winter he would get a two or three months' sentence for vagrancy in those jails. "Or I might go South for the cold weather," he said, "keeping away from the towns where they're horstyle." Now I had learned that where they are hostile they are "horstyle" in tramp talk. He had a slick tongue and a fast way of talking, and soon I walked away, leaving him where he lay on the green grass looking at the blue sky. I would have felt sorry for him if he wasn't so sure he could take care of himself.

During a heavy rainstorm that night I slept in the dry cellar of a house the carpenters hadn't finished and I was up and out before they came to work. I had a fifteen-cent breakfast, found an old tomato can, bought a cheap brush, and had the can filled with asphaltum for a few nickels. Then I went from house to house in several blocks and got three jobs blacking stoves that were rusty, earning seventy-five cents, and two jobs where my pay was dinner and supper. I slept again in the house the carpenters hadn't finished and the next day went from house to house and got no jobs with pay brushing asphaltum on rusty

stoves, though I did get breakfast, dinner, and supper for three jobs. The day after I bought a refill of asphaltum, earned three meals and twenty-five cents. The following day was the same as the day before. I found that the housewives were much like those for whom I had poured milk in Galesburg. I found, too, that if I said I was hoping to earn money to go to college they were ready to help me. The trouble was there were not enough rusty stoves.

Carl Sandburg was born in 1878 in Galesburg, Illinois. He became one of America's most important twentieth-century poets, known for celebrating the beauty in ordinary lives and ordinary things.

Tales from Tornado Alley

WILLIAM LEAST HEAT-MOON

No collection of prairie literature would be complete without at least one tornado story. This one comes from William Least Heat-Moon's book PrairyErth, *an exploration of Chase County, Kansas.*

The Evanses are in their early seventies but appear a decade younger, their faces shaped by the prairie wind into strong and pleasing lines. They have no children. Paul speaks softly and to the point, and Leola is animated, the kind of woman who can take a small, smoldering story and breathe it into bright flame. Paul listens to her in barely noticeable amusement and, from time to time, tosses her tinder. The meal is a Charolais roast beef from their herd, mashed potatoes, pickled beets and candied cucumbers, and Paul's specialty, cottage cheese dressed with corn syrup, and I have two helpings of each but for the last. I've been in the field all day, and it was cold, and, in all my time in the county, I've been asked to join a meal only a few times. We sit happily and there is time for stories.

Leola says: *It was 1949, May. Paul was home from the Pacific. We'd made it through the war, then this. We were living just across the county line, near Americus, on a little farm by the Neosho River. One Friday night I came upstairs to bed and Paul gawked at me. He said, "What the dickens are you doing?" I was wearing my good rabbit fur* coat and wedding rings, and I had a handful of wooden matches. It wasn't cold at all. I said I didn't know but that something wasn't right, and he said, "What's not right?" and I didn't know. We went to bed and just after dark it began to rain, and then the wind came on and blew harder, and we went downstairs and tried to open the door but the air pressure was so strong Paul couldn't even turn the knob. That wind had us locked in. We hunkered in the corner of the living room in just our pajamas—mine were new seersucker—and me in my fur coat. The wind got louder, then the windows blew out, and we realized we were in trouble when the heat stove went around the corner and out a wall that had just come down. We clamped on to each other like ticks, and then we were six feet in the air, and Paul was hanging on to my fur coat—for ballast he says now—and we went up and out where the wall had been, and then we came down, and then we went up again, longer this time, and then came down in a heap of animals—a cow and one of our dogs with a two-by-four through it. The cow lived, but we lost the dog. We were out in the wheat field, sixty yards from the house, and Paul had a knot above his eye that made him look like the Two-headed Wonder Boy. Splintered wood and glass and metal all over, and the electric lines down and sparking, and here we were barefoot. Paul said to walk only when the lightning flashed to see what we were stepping on. We were more afraid of getting electrocuted than cut. We could see in the flashes that the second story of the house was gone except for one room, and we saw the car was an accordion and our big truck was up-side down. The old hog was so terrified she got between us and wouldn't leave all the way up to the neighbors'. Their place wasn't touched. They came to the door and saw a scared hog and two things in rags covered with black mud sucked up out of the river and coated with plaster dust and blood, and one of them was growing a second head. The neighbors didn't know who we were until they heard our voices.

Paul says, *That tornado was on a path to miss our house until it hit* the Neosho and veered back on us. *The Indians believed a twister will change course when it crosses a river.*

Leola: *The next morning we walked back home. The electric clock was stopped at nine-forty, and I went upstairs to the one room that was left, and, there on the chest, my glasses were just like I left them, but our bedroom was gone, and our mattress, all torn up, was in a tree where we'd have been.*

Paul: *We spit plaster for three weeks. It was just plain embedded in us.*

I'm thinking, what truer children of Kansas than those taken aloft by the South Wind?

〜

William Trogdon, *who writes under the name William Least Heat-Moon, was born of English-Irish-Osage ancestry in Kansas City, Missouri, in 1939. He is the author of* PrairyErth (a deep map), River Horse, *and* Blue Highways.

Dakota Thunderstorm

LAURENCE SNYDAL

Black, bruise blue, purple, stonewall-prison gray,
Morning clouds crowd between high heaven's brow
And the bluff where bison died. I see how
This storm storms the prairie. I know the way
Wet weather works. I see how quickly day
Descends to dark, how pressure pulls its plow
Through shocked air, how grain and grass will bend, bow
And bend when the storm comes marching. I stay
In. The sun sinks. Water walks on baled hay.
Light links low and high. Light links here and now.
Light leads loud down to where my ears allow
It entrance. Then at last the rain will lay
Its hard hand on the roof and I stand under
Lightning's neat knife, hammer blows of thunder.

Laurence Snydal *is a poet, musician, and professional cook. His poetry has appeared in such magazines as* Blue Unicorn, Caperock, Lyric, *and* Gulf Stream. *He has published two nonfiction books, both of which are guides for new fathers. A long-time resident of San José, California, he grew up in Williston, North Dakota.*

From Thin Air

DOUGLAS C. DOSSON

This story is based on a legend that the author's grandmother told to him and his sister at bedtime when they were young.

Lisa Jensen held up the purple yarn and carefully examined it. It was perfect, and Lisa imagined how beautiful the yarn would look when woven into a pattern on a white sweater or a yellow blanket. The cool breeze coming through the open window of the Jensens' small farmhouse reminded Lisa that autumn had arrived on the plains of South Dakota. But she didn't mind. That summer of 1913 had been a good one and Lisa was looking forward to selling the summer's produce at the fall market in Huron.

The Jensens had immigrated from Scandinavia eight years earlier. Lisa's father raised some of the finest sheep in the area with the help of her brother, Karl, who was fifteen. Although Lisa helped some with those chores, her main contribution was taking the sheeps' wool and creating woven goods to sell at the market.

Lisa loved spinning, dyeing, and weaving the wool from the Jensens' sheep. She had a keen eye for detail and a creative mind when it came to weaving elaborate patterns into each item she made. Even though she was only fourteen years old,

Lisa was already well known for her sweaters, scarves, and blankets. Each fall she could count on selling every article she had made, and this year she already had four big boxes filled with her woolen goods ready for market.

A distant bell began to clang, breaking Lisa's concentration on her work. It was noon, and the clanging of the Makinens' huge dinner bell rang out across the plains as if it were only next door instead of half a mile down the road.

Lisa moved her skeins of freshly dyed yarn from the kitchen table to the bench by the window and got down the big stoneware bowls from the cupboard. A pot of vegetable soup had been simmering on the stove all morning. As Lisa spooned it out into the bowls she could already hear the rattling of the old wagon and the snorting of Chester and Blackie, Dad's two big workhorses, as the wagon pulled up out front. Then there was the sound of the handle of the small hand pump outside as Dad and Karl washed up. Finally the door swung open and the two clomped into the house.

"Hello, Lisa," they greeted.

"That soup smells good," Dad said.

"Yes, and I'm really hungry!" Karl added.

Karl was *always* hungry, Lisa thought. It amazed her how much he had grown in the past year. She remembered when she and Karl had been the same size. But now, as he sat there at the table, he was almost as big as Dad. Lisa couldn't help but notice, also, that the beautiful sweater she had made for him just last March, which had fit him nicely then, was already getting tight.

The Jensens enjoyed their meal and talked about the upcoming trip to the market and the things they might buy if the market was good.

Then Lisa's dad broke in with a serious instruction. "Karl," he said, "you'd better herd the sheep down to the windmill tank for a drink this afternoon. It feels like a storm is on its way, so we'll need to get them all into the barn before nightfall."

"First thing after lunch," Karl promised.

"How's *your* work going, Lisa?" Dad asked.

"Good," she said. "When you come up for supper, I should have all my new skeins dyed and ready to show you."

"Let's get back to it then," Dad said, pushing himself away from the table.

Karl stood up too and turned to follow his dad outside. As he did, Lisa saw something that made her gasp. "Karl!" she cried. "Come here."

"What is it?" Karl asked.

"Look at this," she said, taking him by the wrist. "You've torn the end of your sweater and it's starting to unravel."

Karl looked at the three inches of yarn dangling down from his wrist. "Oh, it'll be all right," he said.

"No," Lisa insisted. "Let me pin it until you come in tonight. Otherwise that whole sweater could completely unravel."

The sweater had been specially made by Lisa for her brother—hand knitted, not woven—and she pinned the unraveling yarn very carefully as Karl watched.

When she was finally done, Karl flashed her a boyish grin. "Thanks," he said. "But you could always make me a new sweater."

"Get out of here before I make you *buy* one at the market." Lisa shook her head as she watched him leave. Karl was big like a man, but he was still a boy in so many ways.

Lisa cleared the table and got right back to her work. She began laying out the pattern for two matching scarves for an old woman from Aberdeen and immediately became absorbed in the project. She must have worked for two or three hours when an unexpected noise broke the silence of the September air. It was the clanging of the Makinens' bell again.

That's strange, Lisa thought. It's much too early for supper. She went to the window and listened. The pealing of the bell went on and on. The rule of the prairie was that bells were rung only as a reminder of mealtime or to signal an emergency. There must be some kind of trouble, Lisa thought.

She raced out the door and ran all the way to the Makinens'. "What is it?" Lisa called as she came within shouting distance of Mrs. Makinen.

"Something's happened at the windmill," Mrs. Makinen called back.

"Karl!" Lisa cried, remembering that her brother was down at the windmill. She turned and ran.

When Lisa was within a quarter mile of the windmill, she could see her dad and two other men standing by the water tank underneath it. The huge windmill pumped all the water for the cattle and sheep of the area. Lisa saw a fourth man, who looked like Ivan Fernelius, jump onto a horse and gallop off to the northeast.

"What's happened?" Lisa cried as she approached.

"It's your brother," her father told her. "He's stuck up there at the top of the windmill."

Lisa looked up. Sure enough, there was Karl perched on the tiny platform at the very top of the seventy-five-foot windmill frame. "What's he doing up there?" Lisa gasped.

"He must have climbed up to look for stray sheep," Arnie Makinen said. "Then the ladder must've broken away and fallen down."

Lisa looked down and saw that the old wooden ladder, which had once extended up one side of the windmill tower, was now lying on the ground and splintered into dozens of pieces.

"Now there's no way to get him down," Isaac Johnson added.

He was right, for the windmill was constructed of very simple angle-iron framing that made it impossible to climb up or down without a ladder, and the old wooden one was so badly broken it could never be repaired.

Lisa looked up at her brother clinging to the tiny platform. Dark storm clouds were moving in quickly from the west. Her father couldn't hide his worry.

"We sent Toivo to Huron to try to talk the fire department into bringing out their hook and ladder truck," he explained. "But there's no way we'll know if he had any luck."

"And Ivan Fernelius headed for Hitchcock to try to find the construction company that built his barn," Arnie Makinen added. "They have some extension ladders, but who knows where they're working now?"

"The worst thing," Isaac Johnson said, pointing west, "is that the storm's coming in so fast. Feel how the wind is picking up. Karl will never be able to hold on up there when the storm hits the top of that windmill."

Lisa stared back up at poor Karl on his tenuous perch. The wind was already so strong that it was turning the windmill wheel at a torrid rate. She looked up at the thick, black storm clouds rapidly approaching from the west. It was a desperate situation and something had to be done.

Then Lisa had an idea. "Do you have any ropes?" she asked.

"We have plenty of ropes," Isaac Johnson said. "But no way to get them up to Karl."

"I think I know a way to get a rope to him," Lisa said, and she moved out into the open where Karl could see her clearly. The noise of the wind roaring through the windmill wheel so close to Karl's head made it impossible for him to hear her. Lisa could only communicate with hand signals. She waved up at Karl and he waved back in acknowledgment. She held both arms high over her head and pointed emphatically to her left wrist. Then she made a tumbling motion with her hands.

Karl stared down for several moments as Lisa repeated this gesture over and over. Finally, Karl seemed to understand and began to do something with his wrist.

"What are you doing, Lisa?" her father asked.

"The sleeve of Karl's sweater is torn," Lisa said. "I pinned it up at lunchtime. If Karl starts at that point and unravels the yarn from his sweater, he can drop it down to us. I can tie a rope onto the end of the yarn and he can pull the rope back up with that. See," Lisa said, pointing, "the yarn is already starting to come down."

When the men squinted and looked up toward the top of the windmill, they could, in fact, see a tiny string of yarn hanging over the edge of the platform.

"But Lisa," Arnie Makinen asked, "will the yarn be strong enough to hoist a rope back up?"

"I spun that yarn myself," Lisa said. "It should be strong enough. We might have to use a smaller rope first and then hoist a bigger one with that. But my yarn should not break."

"And you think it will be long enough to reach all the way down here?" Isaac Johnson asked.

"There's over three hundred yards of yarn in that sweater," Lisa said. "There will be enough to reach the ground before

Karl's halfway done unraveling. But we have to hurry," Lisa added. "Look at that sky!"

She was right. The sky was now completely black and the west wind had reached thirty miles per hour. The yarn was carried far out away from the windmill tower as it slowly came down, down, down, until Lisa could finally reach the end of it. Quickly, she and her father tied the smallest rope to the yarn and signaled to Karl at the top of the windmill. Then they all held their breath as Karl began to pull the rope back up. They knew that there was no longer any chance that either the hook and ladder truck from the fire department or the extension ladders from the construction company would arrive on time. Lisa's plan was Karl's only hope.

Lisa's yarn strained under the weight of the rope and the stress of the west wind and it stretched dangerously thin. But it did not break. Everyone let out a sigh of relief as the rope reached the platform at the top of the windmill.

With the rain pellets beginning to fall in the driving wind, Karl pulled the heavier rope up and tied it tightly to the angle iron on the platform. Then, fighting the gale, he carefully climbed onto the rope and wrapped his long legs around it. Lisa and her dad and the other two men all held the rope at the bottom to keep it from waving back and forth in the fierce wind. Then Karl slowly slid the seventy-five feet down to the ground where he was greeted with hugs and handshakes.

But even before the greetings had subsided, Karl turned to his sister.

"Thanks a lot, Lisa," he said. Then he looked back up to the top of the windmill where the wind, now well over forty miles an hour, was shaking the platform from which he had come and pelting it with huge raindrops. "I think you saved my life."

Lisa ran her fingers over what was left of his sweater. "Looks like I'll be making you a new sweater after all," she said with a smile. She reached up and hugged him hard.

⌣

Douglas C. Dosson *is the probate and juvenile judge of Roscommon County, Michigan. He is also a writer of children's stories. His published works include* Cody's Wooden Whistle *(Meadowbrook Press) and* Tricking the Wolves *(Meadowbrook Press).*

Great Places

How to Live
in Buffalo County

DON WELCH

Bless the wind.

Listen to at least
three languages:
the county's, the township's,
your house.

Love distance like
a loon, read stones,
make wildflowers
familiar.

Live in this place,
hoping to get there.

Don Welch *is a native Nebraskan who has taught both poetry and*
philosophy at the University of Nebraska at Kearney. He has also been
a visiting poet in the public schools for twenty-five years.

Springtime on the Plains

Hal Borland

Between the ages of ten and fifteen, Hal Borland lived on a ranch near what is now Woodrow, Colorado. In this excerpt from his memoir, High, Wide and Lonesome, *he describes the long-awaited arrival of spring to his High Plains home.*

On that boundless open grassland neither Spring nor any other season can hide or creep up slowly. Spring comes in a vast green wave rolling northward, a wave as evident as were the buffalo millions that once swept northward with new grass, as evident as the Winter-hungry Indians that once swept northward with the buffalo. Spring on the plains has little more subtlety than a thunder storm.

Winter ends, March drags its cold, muddy feet but finally passes, and there is Spring, a rebirth that assaults all your senses. The surge of life at the grass roots penetrates your soles, creeps up through your bones, your marrow, and right into your heart. You see it, you feel it, you smell it, you taste it in every breath you breathe. You partake of Spring. You are a part of it, even as you were a part of Winter. Spring is all around you and in you, primal, simple as the plains them-selves. Spring is, and you know it.

I rode over to the Bromleys to return "David Copperfield"

and get "A Tale of Two Cities." Mr. Bromley said, "Well, it looks like Spring is really coming, at last. Is it always this late?"

I told him that Spring had been early last year, and the year before.

"Back home in Illinois," he said, "the farmers are already out plowing. And the robins are back. Aren't there any robins out here?"

"Not out here," I said. "There are robins near Brush, but not out here. The horned larks are back, though. I saw a couple of them this morning."

"Horned larks?" Mrs. Bromley asked.

I described them.

"Oh," she said, "those little birds. Remember, Walter, I said they must be our equivalent of the English skylarks? They fly high in the air, singing as they fly. Last Fall I sometimes heard them singing when they were so high I could scarcely see them."

"They're the ones," I said. "The big red ants are getting busy, too. And last night, just before dark, I saw two big flocks of geese go over."

"Seems late to me," Mr. Bromley said. "I still miss the robins."

On the way home I saw a badger cleaning out his den. He was down in the hole kicking dirt out with his hind feet almost as fast as a man could toss it out with a shovel. Then I saw a flock of meadow larks. Most of them were busy looking for beetles, but two of them were so full of song they just strutted around whistling at each other. And when I got to the head of our draw I saw the first of the lark buntings, which we called prairie bobolinks. Half a dozen of them flew up, singing on the wing, and I knew that before long I would be finding their nests in the grass, and light blue eggs in the nests.

A few days later I rode over to the big prairie dog town. Even there, where the prairie dogs had eaten the soil bare last Summer, the grass was beginning to come back. The prairie dogs were out by the hundred, chipper and noisy as though they hadn't an enemy in the world. Over at the far side of the town an old badger was waddling along, watching me over one shoulder. The dogs over there were all out of sight, but a hundred yards from the badger other prairie dogs paid him no attention.

Two little owls were bobbing and screaming at each other; they saw me and forgot their own quarrel and screamed at me, but the minute I was past they began hopping at each other again.

Most of the old mother prairie dogs were fat with pup. The pups would be born in another week or two, but would stay in the dens for a month. The thin old males were feeding greedily on the grass, truculent and quarrelsome among themselves.

I dismounted to watch an ant hill, and I saw two tumble-bugs pushing each other around in the grass. They butted and rolled and nipped and got to their feet and butted each other again, until one of them drove the other off. The victor pursued a little way, then came back and began rolling the ball of dung over which they probably had been fighting. They were strange creatures with the mark of antiquity on them, though I didn't know then that they were close cousins of the ancient Egyptian scarabs. All I knew was that these big, dark, timeless looking beetles fashioned balls of cow manure three-quarters of an inch in diameter and rolled them from place to place, walking backward and rolling the balls with their hind legs. They laid eggs in the balls and the eggs hatched into grubs which ate their way out and eventually turned into beetles which laid their own eggs in other dung balls. It seemed to me that the way the birds did it, laying eggs in nests, eggs with shells on them and food inside, was much simpler.

I watched the tumblebug maneuver his ball to the edge of the bare space around the ant hill, and I watched the ants gather to repel the invader, who paid almost no attention to them. The tumblebug rolled his ball across the little clearing and into the grass beyond, the ants rubbed feelers in a conference as though telling each other that they had driven off a major threat to the colony, and everybody went back to work.

The sun was warm. Even the ground was beginning to lose its March chill. I lay there thinking about the beetles and the ants and the prairie dogs and the badgers and the owls and the meadow larks. They had been here a long time, all of them. They were here when the buffalo first came, and that was so long ago that the Indians couldn't remember that far back. Time was a strange thing. It was days and nights and months and years, and then it stretched out into something else. Into grass, maybe, or into clouds. Or into the earth itself. You lay watching a cloud overhead, and you closed your eyes and pretty soon the cloud moved over the sun. You felt the coolness and the darkness of the shadow. You lay and waited for the brightness and the sun's warmth again. You could count, slowly, and that was time. You counted slowly, and the cloud passed the sun. The shadow was gone.

Time was strange. A prairie dog pup was born in May, and by Fall it was practically grown up. A meadow lark laid an egg in a nest in May and before frost in the Fall the baby bird hatched from that egg was as big as its mother and it flew south with the other birds. But it took years for a boy to grow up.

We had been out there two years. When we first came I was so short I had to stand on a manger or a cut-bank to get on a horse. Now I could mount Mack from the ground, just put my hands on his withers and jump and throw my leg over his back.

I wondered how many ants had grown old and died while I was growing up enough to get on a horse from the ground. A year must be a long time to an ant. Or a beetle. Or a prairie dog. Even a day must be a long time. Maybe time was like distance. If an ant got twenty feet away from the ant hill he was a long way from home, much farther than I was right now from the house. And it probably would take a tumblebug all day to roll that ball of dung fifty feet, especially with all the obstacles it had to get over or around.

Some day, I told myself, I would find a tumblebug early in the morning and watch him all day and see just how far he did go. I would catch him and tie a thread around him, or mark him some way, so I could be sure to know which one he was if he had a fight with another beetle.

But not today. I caught Mack and whistled to Fritz, who was still trying to catch a prairie dog, and I rode west, to circle back toward our place.

I rode only a little way when a kit fox jumped not fifty yards ahead of me. He had been catching ground squirrels until I startled him. A kit fox was like a small coyote with a very bushy tail. He was really a fox, but not much bigger than a good-sized cat. There weren't many of them around, and most of them were here on these South Flats. This one jumped and ran like a streak, its bushy tail floating behind, graceful as a bird. It ran maybe twenty yards; then, without slackening pace, it veered and ran off at an angle another twenty-five yards or so, then changed directions again. That's the way a kit fox always ran, zigzag. Dogs would seldom run kit foxes, and anyone who ever watched one knew why. It made you dizzy just watching that zigzagging. I yelled, and the kit veered again. One more turn and it vanished in a little hollow.

I rode over to the hollow, but I couldn't find the kit fox. It must have darted down the little wash and out onto the flats again where I wasn't watching. But as I rode down the hollow I came to a fresh cut-bank that had washed out in the Spring melt. The grass had caved away leaving a bank of fresh gravelly soil. Such a place was always worth searching for arrowheads. I got off and began poking through the gravel.

It was different from the gravel on our land, coarser and full of lumps of sandstone. The sandstone was grayish yellow. There was a thin ledge of it reaching back under the grass. I sifted a few handfuls through my fingers and stood up, about to leave. Then I scuffed at it with my toe and a smooth, rounded flat piece caught my eye. It wasn't a pebble. It was almost the size of a silver dollar, but smooth and rounded.

Even as I picked it up I sensed that here was something out of time so remote that my mind could not quite grasp the distance. It was a fossil clam, and the place I found it was fifteen hundred miles from the nearest ocean.

There it was, a clam turned to stone, a petrified clam with fluting around the edges of the twin shells, with bits of sandstone still clinging to it. Different from the fresh-water clams of the Missouri river, but still a shellfish, something from an ocean that once had been where I stood. And somehow, standing in the warm Spring sunlight on the high plains, I comprehended the matter of eons and ages. Without knowing geology, I sensed geologic time. I touched the beat of the big rhythm, the coming and going of oceans and the rise and fall of mountains. And, for a little while, I was one not only with the Indians who had been there before me, but with those who were there before the Indians; not only with the grass which had greened with a thousand Springs, but with that which was there before the grass.

There had been ranchmen before we came, and Indians before the ranchmen, and buffalo before the Indians. And long before the buffalo there had been an ocean, and clams. Back, back—how far back? And how far ahead? Time was indeed a strange thing. The time of the ant, the time of the tumblebug, the time of the prairie dog, the time of a boy. The time of a fossil clam.

I got on my horse and rode slowly home in the late afternoon of that Spring day, with a strange, hard, smooth fragment of time in my pocket.

Mother said, "You've just got time to get the chores done before supper."

❧

Hal Borland *was born in 1900 and spent much of his life observing and writing about the natural world. A columnist for the* New York Times, *he was also the author of more than a dozen books for children and adults.*

Ice Whales

Joyce Sidman

At the edge of the lake,
I step out onto a place
I can't go in summer.
My boots crunch on the foot-thick ice.
Long blue cracks
spider off into nowhere.
I follow deer prints,
climb the frozen muskrat lodge.
The wind whistles.
The shore looks far away.

Then I hear it,
weird and wonderful,
like the call of some giant beast:
the lake ice is
singing with cold.
It sounds like whales,
ice whales,
deep in the silvery dark.
I place my mittened hands
palm down and listen:

Welcome, they call,
to this special place,
this frozen world,
after the long summer.

Joyce Sidman *lives with her husband and two sons in Wayzata, Minnesota, where she walks every day with her dog, Merlin. She is the author of* Just Us Two: Poems about Animal Dads *(Millbrook Press) and a book of adult poetry. She also writes a regular column for the* St. Paul Pioneer Press.

The Last Best Swimming Hole

PATRIC ROWLEY

On hot summer days, some prairie inhabitants nestle in their burrows, some curl up under rocks, and others seek out a cool, tree-lined river.

Between 1932 and 1942 the rivers that split and ran through Wichita were sweet and clean and perfect for swimming. For my money, the best swimming hole of all was on the east bank of the Little River at about Eighteenth Street.

There was a small beach that eased into the water. You could wade to any depth you chose. The main channel near the west bank was the deepest spot. The riverbank behind the beach was steep and thickly covered by bushes and clumps of willows and a heavy stand of cane.

It was not possible to see the Eighteenth Street swimming hole from Arkansas Avenue, the street that ran alongside. The policemen who came to enforce the ordinance that made swimming in the river illegal had to walk down the narrow trail and through the brush just like we did.

Wichita was hot and dry back in the '30s. There was no television, not much on the radio in summer, very little money for movies, and only a few overregulated public pools with freezing water and arrogant bullies for lifeguards.

There was no air-conditioning to speak of, certainly not in

our homes. Only the very affluent had even electric fans. Mostly you saw old ladies fanning themselves with large palm-shaped fans on a stick. These were given away as advertisements for feed stores and mortuaries. With all the heat and the boredom from having nowhere to go and no money to spend, the lure of the river was irresistible; already by noon a

dozen or so people would be in the water at our Eighteenth Street congregating place. By three, the crowd would reach forty to fifty.

The culture was intergenerational and interracial. Even though our schools were segregated through the first eight grades and African Americans had to sit in the balconies of "white" motion-picture theaters, democracy was practiced very quietly and very efficiently down on the river at Eighteenth Street.

Adults came to Eighteenth Street, too. They were, for the most part, women with children too young to swim. The mothers would wade in wearing their dresses, holding their children's hands. Grown men would roll up the legs of their overalls and stand in the cool water. Most of the swimming garb was catch-as-catch-can. In a nation and city of poor people, we generally represented the poorest of the poor. Under certain circumstances, even underwear was all right.

The water on Eighteenth Street was always warm and friendly and inviting. You had to go deep in the main channel to find a cold current. A crude diving platform was nailed twenty feet up into a huge cottonwood tree right on the edge of the river. A heavy rope swing hung down from a limb just below it.

No one was in charge at the Eighteenth Street swimming club. Actually, it wasn't even a club. It was more like a hobo jungle. A calm, quiet, secret place where anyone could find soft breezes, cool water, silky sand, and a haven from the rough, raw edges of reality.

Those of us who hung around the swimming hole had only a casual access to the more refined uses of the river. On our way to the free park shows—shaky, grainy silent westerns shown outdoors near the Riverside Zoo—we would see the motor launch leaving the boathouse for an excursion up the river. Most of the people aboard were dressed in white and pink and were wearing straw hats. They didn't look like our parents. Rich people.

A lot of the children belonging to the people who rode the big, slick, mahogany motor launch had their own slick canoes, which they languidly paddled around in the middle of the river off Back Bay Boulevard, as if it were their own private pond. Rich kids.

When the summer nights got so hot during the mid-'30s that even porches and backyards could no longer keep people cool enough to sleep through the night, they came to the river with their blankets and sheets and slept on the banks.

The rivers in those days seemed to have something for everybody. To boys like me, they were marvelous places to explore, to dream, and to discover. I could not have found a better passage into understanding what a kind and gentle place the world can be if you don't push it too hard.

~

Patric Rowley *is a painter, teacher, and writer who still makes his home in Wichita. He and his wife, Betty, edit and publish several aviation magazines. They have been married for almost fifty years.*

The Country of Grass

WILLA CATHER

Willa Cather's 1917 novel, My Ántonia, *portrays the lives of early Nebraska settlers, including Jim Burden and Ántonia, his childhood friend. In this excerpt Jim, recently orphaned and sent to live with his grandparents, describes his first impressions of his grandparents' farm and the surrounding prairie.*

Early the next morning I ran out-of-doors to look about me. I had been told that ours was the only wooden house west of Black Hawk—until you came to the Norwegian settlement, where there were several. Our neighbours lived in sod houses and dugouts—comfortable, but not very roomy. Our white frame house, with a storey and half-storey above the basement, stood at the east end of what I might call the farmyard, with the windmill close by the kitchen door. From the windmill the ground sloped westward, down to the barns and granaries and pig-yards. This slope was trampled hard and bare, and washed out in winding gullies by the rain. Beyond the corncribs, at the bottom of the shallow draw, was a muddy little pond, with rusty willow bushes growing about it. The road from the post-office came directly by our door, crossed the farmyard, and curved round this little pond, beyond which it began to climb the gentle swell of unbroken prairie to the west. There, along the western sky-line, it skirted a great cornfield, much larger than any field I had ever seen. This cornfield, and the sorghum patch behind the barn, were the only broken land in sight. Everywhere, as far as the eye could reach, there was nothing but rough, shaggy, red grass, most of it as tall as I.

North of the house, inside the ploughed fire-breaks, grew a thick-set strip of box-elder trees, low and bushy, their leaves already turning yellow. This hedge was nearly a quarter of a mile long, but I had to look very hard to see it at all. The little trees were insignificant against the grass. It seemed as if the grass were about to run over them, and over the plum-patch behind the sod chicken-house.

As I looked about me I felt that the grass was the country, as the water is the sea. The red of the grass made all the great prairie the colour of wine-stains, or of certain seaweeds when they are first washed up. And there was so much motion in it; the whole country seemed, somehow, to be running.

I had almost forgotten that I had a grandmother, when she came out, her sunbonnet on her head, a grain-sack in her hand, and asked me if I did not want to go to the garden with her to dig potatoes for dinner.

The garden, curiously enough, was a quarter of a mile from the house, and the way to it led up a shallow draw past the cattle corral. Grandmother called my attention to a stout hickory cane, tipped with copper, which hung by a leather thong from her belt. This, she said, was her rattlesnake cane. I must never go to the garden without a heavy stick or a corn-knife; she had killed a good many rattlers on her way back and forth. A little girl who lived on the Black Hawk road was bitten on the ankle and had been sick all summer.

I can remember exactly how the country looked to me as I walked beside my grandmother along the faint wagon tracks on that early September morning. Perhaps the glide of long railway travel was still with me, for more than anything else I felt motion in the landscape; in the fresh, easy-blowing morning wind, and in the earth itself, as if the shaggy grass were a sort of loose hide, and underneath it herds of wild buffalo were galloping, galloping. . . .

Alone, I should never have found the garden—except, perhaps, for the big yellow pumpkins that lay about unprotected by their withering vines—and I felt very little interest in it when I got there. I wanted to walk straight on through the red grass and over the edge of the world, which could not be very far away. The light air about me told me that the world ended here: only the ground and sun and sky were left, and if one went a little farther there would be only sun and sky, and one would float off into them, like the tawny hawks which sailed over our heads making slow shadows on the grass. While grandmother took the pitchfork we found standing in one of the rows and dug potatoes, while I picked them up out of the soft brown earth and put them into the bag, I kept looking up at the hawks that were doing what I might so easily do.

When grandmother was ready to go, I said I would like to stay up there in the garden awhile.

She peered down at me from under her sunbonnet. "Aren't you afraid of snakes?"

"A little," I admitted, "but I'd like to stay, anyhow."

"Well, if you see one, don't have anything to do with him. The big yellow and brown ones won't hurt you; they're bull-snakes and help to keep the gophers down. Don't be scared if you see anything look out of that hole in the bank over there.

That's a badger hole. He's about as big as a big 'possum, and his face is striped, black and white. He takes a chicken once in a while, but I won't let the men harm him. In a new country a body feels friendly to the animals. I like to have him come out and watch me when I'm at work."

Grandmother swung the bag of potatoes over her shoulder and went down the path, leaning forward a little. The road followed the windings of the draw; when she came to the first bend, she waved at me and disappeared. I was left alone with this new feeling of lightness and content.

I sat down in the middle of the garden, where snakes could scarcely approach unseen, and leaned my back against a warm yellow pumpkin. There were some ground-cherry bushes growing along the furrows, full of fruit. I turned back the papery triangular sheaths that protected the berries and ate a few. All about me giant grasshoppers, twice as big as any I had ever seen, were doing acrobatic feats among the dried vines. The gophers scurried up and down the ploughed ground. There in the sheltered draw-bottom the wind did not blow very hard, but I could hear it singing its humming tune up on the level, and I could see the tall grasses wave. The earth was warm under me, and warm as I crumbled it through my fingers. Queer little red bugs came out and moved in slow squadrons around me. Their backs were polished vermilion, with black spots. I kept as still as I could. Nothing happened. I did not expect anything to happen. I was something that lay under the sun and felt it, like the pumpkins, and I did not want to be anything more. I was entirely happy.

Perhaps we feel like that when we die and become a part of something entire, whether it is sun and air, or goodness and knowledge. At any rate, that is happiness; to be dissolved into something complete and great. When it comes to one, it comes as naturally as sleep.

Born in Virginia in 1873, **Willa Cather** *moved to Nebraska when she was nine. She began writing stories and essays at the University of Nebraska before publishing such celebrated novels as* O Pioneers!, My Ántonia, Shadows on the Rock, *and* Death Comes for the Archbishop.

Letter from Texas

GEORGIA O'KEEFFE

In the early 1900s, artist Georgia O'Keeffe had a long-running friend-ship and correspondence with a fellow artist by the name of Anita Pollitzer. She wrote this letter to Anita after moving to Canyon, Texas, following the death of her mother and an ensuing bout of depression. O'Keeffe signed the letter "Pat," a name used by some of her close friends.

11 September 1916

Tonight I walked into the sunset—to mail some letters—the whole sky—and there is so much of it out here—was just blazing—and grey blue clouds were riding all through the holiness of it—and the ugly little buildings and windmills looked great against it

But some way or other I didn't seem to like the redness much so after I mailed the letters I walked home—and kept walking—

The Eastern sky was all grey blue—bunches of clouds—different kinds of clouds—sticking around everywhere and the whole thing—lit up—first in one place—then in another with flashes of lightning—sometimes just sheet lightning—and some times sheet lightning with a sharp bright zigzag flashing across it—. I walked out past the last house—past the last locust tree—and sat on the fence for a long time—looking—just looking at—the lightning—you see there was nothing but sky and flat prairie land—land that seems more like the ocean than anything else I know—There was a wonderful moon.

Well I just sat there and had a great time all by myself—Not even many night noises—just the wind—

I wondered what you are doing—

It is absurd the way I love this country—Then when I came back—it was funny—roads just shoot across blocks anywhere—all the houses looked alike—and I almost got lost—I had to laugh at myself—I couldnt tell which house was home—

I am loving the plains more than ever it seems—and the SKY—Anita you have never seen SKY—it is wonderful—

Pat.

◞‿◟

Born in 1887, **Georgia O'Keeffe** *was a prominent American artist best known for her paintings of flowers, desert landscapes, and other natural forms.*

Reflections on Gullies

ART BETTIS

The Loess Hills of western Iowa are dome-shaped hills made up of wind-blown deposits of silt. Cutting through these hills are deep ravines, known as gullies, which author Art Bettis explores in this essay.

The gully next to our house in Sioux City was the last frontier in my ten-year-old universe. The deep dark gash through our neighborhood harbored a Loess Hills jungle filled with curious sounds, seldom-seen creatures, and earthy smells that enchanted the boy who inhabited the other world beyond the gully's edge. What made that sound and rippled the water? Would the phantom slither from the gully and into our house at night?

When exploration of the gully finally became reality, the phantom turned out to be turtles, minnows, birds, muskrats, and a host of other creatures that were at home in the thread of wildness winding through the city. Almost every day the world of moms and dads, houses and schools faded rapidly from consciousness as the Cook Street expedition, led by Patty McGraw—the toughest kid on the block—descended the narrow path into the green twilight canyon where discoveries of nature and self abounded. A golden cloud of dust enveloped us as we scrambled down the narrow path clinging to the gully's side. The nearly vertical, forty-foot-high walls of the gully closed around us, and the world above vanished behind an emerald canopy of box elder, silver maple, willow, and elm.

Orioles and robins darted in and out of the trees, box turtles plopped into the tepid water of Perry Creek, and schools of chubs darted to deeper, darker pools as we scampered through the nettle and horseweed jungle on the gully floor. We, too, were creatures of the gully, allied with those that swam, flew, and walked on all fours. In this place, grown-up rules no longer reigned. The gully world had its own rules; getting dirty, muddy, and sometimes wet was inevitable. Anything light enough to move could be thrown into the water, and breaking a bottle bobbing along in the creek moved you up the social ladder. The gully was more than a secluded playground: it was otherworldly, a rarefied blend of earth, organisms, water, and filtered light that diffused through our civilized rind and jostled the wild within.

My interest in the Loess Hills landscape emerged long after I and the other kids on Cook Street grew into adulthood and abandoned Perry Creek's gully. In graduate school, I studied archaeology, soil science, and geology. That's when I met Dave Benn, an archaeologist at a small college who was about to begin an archaeological dig along Held Creek in the Loess Hills near Sioux City. That dig would lead to an awakening in understanding Loess Hills archaeology, present important geologic discoveries, and leave me standing once again in the gully world.

Held Creek's gully looked like thousands of other gullies in northwest Iowa, a ragged seam of cottonwood trees and tall weeds on the monotonous corduroy of the cornfield landscape. Valuable farmland was being destroyed by the advance and widening of the gully, and the Soil Conservation Service was in the process of trying to tame the untamable: building dams to stop the gully's advance, terracing the bordering hills to hold the soil. While examining the project area, an archaeologist had discovered remains of a prehistoric campsite, including bits of pottery, broken and burned deer bones, and a fragment of a ceremonial pipe protruding from a gully wall. Now Dave, ten student archaeologists, and I were going to learn what we could about this ancient camp before it was destroyed by dam construction. So once again I scrambled down a narrow path clinging to a gully's side and entered the gully world, this time searching out phantoms of the deep past.

Cradled deep in the tan-and-black layers of mud in the walls of the gully were clues about the lives of the Hills' prehistoric inhabitants and the position gullies held in their way of life. Centuries before earth lodge villagers congregated in the Glenwood area and along the Little and Big Sioux valleys about a thousand years ago, other Native Americans, known as Plains Woodland Indians by archaeologists, made the Hills their home. These people, who lived in extended families of about ten, made their living by hunting deer, small animals, birds, frogs, and other animals and by searching for insects and plants, all of which would carry them through the seasons in the endless prairie on the eastern edge of the plains. People were not plentiful, and the landscape was rich with resources. Most of the time life was relatively comfortable, but winter must have been another story.

Today's western Iowans know winter: blinding snow coming in horizontal sheets, snow drifts that swallow up cars and paralyze towns, and afterward the "Alberta Clipper"—the deep freeze. Surviving such conditions in a skin-walled hut huddled around a small, open wood fire without down sleeping bags is unimaginable to me. Yet the evidence in Held Creek's gully wall—bits and scraps of pottery and burned deer bone, the orange stain of an extinct fire pit inside a dark lens marking the floor of a dwelling—left no doubt that the hunters did survive winter in the Hills, just as others had done for thousands of previous winters and as their descendants would do for hundreds of winters to come.

This camp was not an isolated occurrence. Layer upon layer of remains were exposed as we dug deeper into the mud of the extinct gully, deeper into time. Soon after the first high Vs of geese passed northward, signaling the approach of spring, the band left its winter camp in the gully. Not long afterward the creek sprung to life, as runoff from melting snow and spring rains trickled down the slopes and rushed into the gully. With the runoff came sediment that sealed the remains of the camp under a new layer of mud, writing another page in the gully's story, part of the chapter on human history. Charcoal from the ancient fire pits we unearthed told us that bands of Woodland hunters stayed here many times between about 1,800 and 1,200 years ago. They stopped visiting this place when the ancient gully was almost filled with sediment, a shallow swale on the valley floor that no longer afforded wood, water, and protection from the winter wind.

Archaeologists now look for and routinely discover remains of the Hills' prehistoric inhabitants exposed in gully walls. During the last fifteen years, the discovery of other prehistoric gully campsites several thousands of years older than the Woodland occupations at Held Creek have opened a new view of past people's relationship with the Loess Hills. Gullies were the winter cornucopia of prehistoric Loess Hills residents. These places provided game, water, wood, and most important, shelter from the relentless wind when winter storms rendered ridges, slopes, and wide valleys off limits to people. Gullies were an essential element in the aboriginal landscape. Yearly movements of the group were planned around the location and characteristics of certain gullies. When a favored gully location finally silted in over the span of several centuries, a younger, deeper gully was sought out for winter stay. To prehistoric inhabitants of the Hills, deep gullies were an asset, nature's gift, beauty.

It's interesting that the landscape can be viewed so differently by different cultures and by different groups in the same culture. Today's environmental problem was the environmental necessity of the past. The unsightly ravine ravaging prime agricultural land was my childhood world of discovery and wonderment, habitat for creatures squeezed off the landscape by human land use, and a window into the past for geologists and archaeologists. Gullies speak to me about some of the consequences of our economy, about the human past and long-term perspectives on the landscape, about the nature of the Hills, about people's place in the environment, about myself. Human arrogance lets some of us believe that we have upset the natural order of things and caused a "gully problem" when, in fact, present gully activity is just one of several gully growth-and-fill episodes that have formed the distinctive landscape of the Loess Hills during the last 20,000 years.

Gullies are a thread in my life. The enchantment I experienced in the gully world as a child emerges again as I stand in the canyons of the Loess Hills, wondering How? When? Why? and awestruck by the human and landscape histories recorded in the sediments of the towering gully walls.

✲

Art Bettis *is an assistant professor in the geosciences department at the University of Iowa in Iowa City.*

Children of the Sun

An Osage Story

In many cultures, creation myths are told to explain the origins of particular places. This Osage myth, which was told by Black Dog to Alice C. Fletcher and Francis La Flesche in the early 1900s, explains the origins of the tallgrass prairie and its inhabitants.

Way beyond (an expression similar to "once upon a time") a part of the Wazha'zhe lived in the sky. They desired to know their origin, the source from which they came into existence. They went to the sun. He told them that they were his children. Then they wandered still farther and came to the moon. She told them that she gave birth to them, and that the sun was their father. She told them that they must leave their present abode and go down to the earth and dwell there. They came to the earth, but found it covered with water. They could not return to the place they had left, so they wept, but no answer came to them from anywhere. They floated about in the air, seeking in every direction for help from some god; but they found none. The animals were with them, and of all these the elk was the finest and most stately, and inspired all the creatures with confidence; so they appealed to the elk for help. He dropped into the water and began to sink. Then he called to the winds and the winds came from all quarters and blew until the waters went upward as in a mist. Before that time the winds traveled only in two directions, from north to south and then back from south to north; but when the elk called they came from the east, the north, the west, and the south, and met at a central point, and carried the water upward.

At first rocks only were exposed, and the people traveled on the rocky places that produced no plants, and there was nothing to eat. Then the waters began to go down until the soft earth was exposed. When this happened the elk in his joy rolled over and over on the soft earth, and all his loose hairs clung to the soil. The hairs grew, and from them sprang beans, corn, potatoes, and wild turnips, and then all the grasses and trees.

The Osage *are Plains Indians who once lived in Illinois, Missouri, and Kansas.*

Prairie Fire

GEORGE CATLIN

Periodic fires once swept across the prairie, stimulating grass growth and preventing trees from taking hold. Later, settlers suppressed the fires to protect their homes and crops. But in this nineteenth-century account, artist George Catlin gives us a glimpse of those early prairie fires.

The burning prairie is one of the most beautiful scenes. Every acre for hundreds and hundreds of miles is grass, which dies and dries, then burns over, leaving the ground a black doleful color.

There are many ways the fire is started either by white men or by Indians by accident, but the fires are often deliberately started to get a fresh crop of grass, for the grazing of horses, or to make easier travelling during the next summer—so there will be no old grass to entangle the feet of man or horse.

Over the elevated prairie bluffs, where the grass is thin and short, the fire slowly creeps with a feeble flame, which one can easily step over. The wild animals often rest in their lairs until the flames almost burn their noses, then reluctantly rise, leap over it, and trot off among the cinders. At night these scenes become indescribably beautiful. The flames are seen many miles, creeping over the sides and tops of the bluffs, sparkling chains of liquid fire hanging suspended in graceful festoons from the skies.

But there is another character of burning prairie, when the grass is seven or eight feet high for many miles on the Missouri bottoms. Then the flames are driven forward by hurricanes which sweep over denuded country. There are many of these meadows on the Missouri, the Platte, and the Arkansas, many miles in breadth, which are perfectly level, with a waving grass so high that we are obliged to stand erect in our stirrups in order to look over its waving tops as we ride through it.

In these, the fire travels at a frightful rate and often destroys parties of Indians on their fleetest horses, if they are so unlucky as to be overtaken by it. It does not travel as fast as a horse at full speed, but the high grass is filled with wild pea-vines and other impediments which render it necessary for the rider to guide his horse in the zigzag paths of the deers and buffaloes, retarding his progress. Then he may be overtaken by the dense column of smoke sweeping before the fire—alarming the horse, which stops and stands terrified, till the burning grass falls about him, kindling up in a moment a thousand new fires, which move on like a black thunder-cloud rolling over the earth, with its lightning's glare and its thunder rumbling as it goes.

George Catlin *traveled across the western prairies and the Rocky Mountains in the early 1800s, painting landscapes and scenes of Indian life. He also published several books of his art and writing, including* Letters and Notes on the North American Indians, *from which this excerpt is drawn.*

Salamander

JAN DONLEY

Although this story is fictional, it is based on Jan Donley's memories of playing near her home in Wyoming and witnessing the changes that occurred to the surrounding prairie.

Kelly watched from her bedroom window as Charlie and Frank rode their bikes up and down Hamilton Way. It was hot. Middle of July. They rode without shirts—just a pair of cutoff denims covered their bodies. Their bare feet hung over the pedals. Kelly thought it was silly, how boys could go around without shirts and girls couldn't. Her eleven-year-old thinking brought her to one startling conclusion: something in this puberty picture seemed unfair.

Just moments earlier, Kelly had been out there with Charlie and Frank, but Charlie kept teasing her. "You're just a girl. Why don't you go inside and play with a doll or something." Charlie used to be her very best friend. He and Kelly went everywhere together—especially on "expeditions" (that's what Charlie called them) into the prairie, just across the street and over the wooden bridge. The prairie stretched out for miles, filled with treasures like horned toads and frogs and hidden ponds—even a junkyard and what might be a haunted house. Lately, though, Charlie was always hanging out with Frank, and somehow, Charlie changed. Suddenly he was calling Kelly a girl and saying she couldn't do the same things boys did.

Charlie and Frank talked about taking a trip to the old junkyard. Charlie said, "We might even sneak inside that old haunted house." It was just the kind of adventure Kelly and Charlie would have taken together. Now, Charlie intended to leave her out in favor of Frank.

"I want to go, too," Kelly said.

"No way," Frank insisted. "Adventures are for boys."

"That's just stupid," Kelly said. After all, the previous summer she and Charlie captured a bunch of tadpoles together, put them in a big bowl with sand and water, and watched them become frogs in Kelly's backyard. Another time, they found an injured horned toad, built a shoe-box home for it, named it Bulldog, and cared for it. Together, they carried it out near the junkyard and set it free. Kelly had participated in these adventures, and many more, in the very same prairie where Charlie and Frank said she didn't belong.

As she watched the boys skid down the street toward the prairie, Kelly knew she had to go, too. She would take the shortcut, get there before them. Just because she was a girl didn't mean she couldn't find her own adventure.

Kelly steered her bike out of her backyard and coasted down the street to the plank that spanned the ditch. Once across, she rode her wide-tired bike through the dirt, making a slalom course out of prickly pears and sagebrush.

She got to the junkyard fast, just in time to hide her bike behind an old stove and crouch down to watch as Frank and Charlie pulled up. Lots of junk littered what appeared to be the prairie yard of a run-down house surrounded by a weathered picket fence. Legend told of a tobacco-chewing ogre who haunted the place, constantly tossing out stoves and refrigerators as if they were paper napkins. Another legend told of a blizzard wind that carried all those appliances here. As anyone who lives in Wyoming knows, those winds can be plenty fierce.

Some people said that no one lived there at all, that it was just an abandoned house, a convenient junkyard site. But Kelly and Charlie knew better. They had seen the shoveled paths in winter and the drawn curtains at twilight. Someone cared for that house.

Kelly watched as Charlie and Frank began poking around the junk; they were trying to pull a rusted handle off some old refrigerator door. Suddenly, the rustle of someone behind her startled Kelly. She turned around to see an old woman holding a great big net.

Kelly was about to scream, but the woman put a finger to her mouth and whispered, "Shhh, those boys'll hear you." Then she squatted next to Kelly, behind the stove.

Kelly caught her breath.

"Name's Sadie. What's the matter, cat got your tongue? What's your name?"

"I'm . . . Kelly, but—"

"Nice to meet you, Kelly. I've seen you before, haven't I?"

"I don't know—I—"

"I'm the ogre that lives in the junkyard house."

"I—"

"You scared of me?"

"Are you gonna catch me in your net?"

Sadie laughed, under her breath, to keep the boys from hearing. "Come with me," she whispered. "Let's get out of their earshot."

Kelly knew she shouldn't go with strangers. She held back.

"Okay." Sadie sensed Kelly's fear. "I'll go. You follow along if you like."

Kelly watched Sadie walk away. She saw that Charlie and Frank had pulled handles off two refrigerator doors and were using them like radio transmitters. Their game looked fun, but she knew she wasn't welcome. Sadie, on the other hand, was eager for Kelly's company. Slowly she went in Sadie's direction.

Just down a small hill, Kelly saw Sadie's back as she kneeled by a tiny pond and ran her net through the water. Kelly knew that pond; it formed in a small valley. Depending on how much rain fell, there was sometimes water, sometimes a muddy hole, and sometimes just cracked dirt. Kelly liked the cracked dirt best because she could pick it up in squares and put it back together, like a puzzle. Kelly watched as Sadie continued to move her net through the water. Then it appeared as if she caught something, for she pulled the net out and said, "Got ya!"

Kelly moved closer still.

Without turning around or skipping a beat, Sadie said, "C'mon, it won't bite."

Kelly peeked over Sadie's shoulder to see a yellow-and-black lizardlike creature in the net. "Wow!" Kelly's fear fell away in the excitement of this discovery. "What's that?"

"Salamander. A six-incher at least. It's a beaut, ain't it?"

"It came from in there?" Kelly pointed at the water.

Sadie nodded. "Sometimes they swim, sometimes they walk on land."

"They can do both? Like frogs?"

"That's right," Sadie said. "There's a word for that: amphibious. That means they can adjust to land or water."

Kelly stared into the net at the creature.

Sadie stared too. "This one's got great colors, that's for sure. And look at those legs, almost like elastic. Did you know that salamanders can lose their legs and grow new ones?"

"No way!"

"It's true," Sadie laughed. "They're very adaptable."

"What are you gonna do with it now that you caught it?"

"I'm gonna paint a picture of it, then I'm gonna set it free."

Kelly followed Sadie back to the house. In fact, she walked right past Charlie and Frank's gaping faces. Their rusted transmitters, not nearly as interesting as Kelly following an old woman into a haunted house, dangled from their hands.

"Hello, boys," Sadie said. "Kelly and I are going in now. You two should be wearing shirts. Don't you know prairie sun can burn you to a crisp?" And with that, Kelly followed Sadie into what was anything but a haunted house. It was magical, full of color. On every wall hung pictures of horned toads, lizards, prairie dogs, chipmunks, prickly pears, sagebrush, and tumbleweeds.

"You're an artist," Kelly said.

Sadie shrugged. "My granddaddy and grandma built this house a hundred years ago. My folks raised me here. Now my home is just a junkyard on the prairie, a nuisance." Sadie pulled a big mason jar down from the kitchen counter and put the salamander in it.

"But it's beautiful in here. It's not a nuisance at all."

Sadie laughed. "Thanks, dear. But the town bought this land from my father just before he died ten years ago. It belongs to the town."

"I don't see how a town can own a home."

"Yeah, it don't make a lot of sense, but it can happen. See all these pictures I've been making? They're my way of holding on to as much of this prairie as I can. I'm not sure it'll be with us much longer."

"The prairie's always gonna be here," Kelly said.

Sadie shook her head. "I used to believe that, too. But it ain't so. Best if we learn to be like this old salamander—grow new feet that can swim and walk." Sadie busied herself collecting paper and pens and watercolors. Kelly watched as she sketched the salamander.

"You're good," Kelly said. She looked at the salamander's eyes staring back at her. "You think it's scared?"

"Who knows? It's quite a compliment to be selected as an artist's model."

Sadie turned her attention to the watercolors and made the yellow-and-black body come to life.

"Wow," Kelly said, "you even made it look shiny."

Kelly wandered the room, looking at all the prairie paintings. She noticed that one of the paintings on the wall was of this house, but the land around it held no stoves or toasters or washing machines—only tall grass and occasional slopes. "Hey, there's no junk in this painting. How come?" Kelly asked.

"This place used to look

just like that picture there," Sadie said as she pointed with her brush. "You've known it only as a junkyard. But that wasn't always the case. People started dumping here about five or six years ago. I can't even keep track. They dump at night. Stuff they don't want. They figure, 'Here's a great big nowhere'—some kind of prairie trash can."

"But it's your yard."

"Used to be my yard. Like I said, the town owns it now. My days are numbered in this house. I heard 'em talking the other day. The big store's been approved. It won't be long before they tear my house down."

"What about all your paintings?"

"They'll come with me. Don't you worry."

"But where?"

"Shoot, girl. All this talk about my house makes me sad." Sadie added some finishing touches to her salamander painting, then signed a yellow "S" along the bottom. "Now, then, how about some iced tea while we wait for the paint to dry?"

Kelly nodded. She was thirsty.

After the tea, Sadie rolled up the now-dry salamander painting, tied a string around it, and handed it to Kelly. "You can have it," Sadie offered.

"I can keep it?" Kelly said.

Sadie nodded. "Consider it a prairie memory—that day you had with the crazy net-lady."

Kelly put the rolled-up tube of paper to her eye and looked through it at the real salamander waiting patiently in the mason jar.

"Now, let's go set Little Miss Salamander free." Sadie lifted the jar and set out through the front door. Kelly followed. She slipped the rolled-up painting into the basket on her bike.

Back at the pond, Kelly and Sadie said good-bye to the salamander.

"There you go, little one," Sadie said. They watched the salamander skitter along the edge of the water, then glide right in. "See that?" Sadie said. "That silly critter knows exactly where to go."

"Can I come back and visit?" Kelly wanted to know.

Sadie kissed Kelly on the cheek. "You can come any time you want, but I can't say for sure where I'll be."

"But your house is here."

Sadie patted Kelly on the shoulder and squinted up at the sky. "Sometimes," she said, "you've got no choice but to hold home inside you somewhere. That way, no one can take it away from you. You go on now, while it's still light out. I bet your mom's calling you for dinner."

Kelly got on her bike, and halfway home she saw Frank and Charlie waiting for her.

"What happened?" Charlie asked.

Kelly shrugged and rode right past them. They followed along.

"Was she a monster?"

"Did she look like a monster to you?" Kelly asked.

"Did she hurt you?"

"No," Kelly said, "she wouldn't hurt anyone."

"Maybe she's a ghost," Charlie speculated.

"Listen." Kelly stopped her bike. "She's my discovery."

"Oh, so Kelly's got a secret," Frank teased.

"Maybe I do, maybe I don't," Kelly said, and she rode away. Before she did, she noticed a smile in Charlie's eyes, and it made her miss him. As if he read her mind, he raced to catch up with her, leaving Frank in the dust.

Once home, Kelly fashioned a frame from some old cardboard, and she put the salamander painting inside. She fell asleep dreaming about how she would visit Sadie again.

Almost a month went by before Kelly could sneak away, and when she got to the junkyard, it was gone. So was the house. All she saw were piles of dirt, old wood, a great big bulldozer, some tractors, and a backhoe. A man in a hard hat told Kelly to back away. "It's dangerous here, kiddo. Your parents know you're here?"

Kelly ran to the pond where she and Sadie had let the salamander go. It had dried up, and all that remained was a muddy hole. Kelly sat there by the mud and cried. Sometimes, discoveries were no fun at all.

Then she remembered what Sadie said: "Hold home somewhere inside you. That way, no one can take it away from you."

Kelly let her eyes wander over the prairie. She kept her gaze straight ahead, where the great big sky looked down on the sage-colored land. If she tried hard enough, she could drown out the sound of those bulldozers in the background and concentrate on the whisper of wind through the tall grass.

Jan Donley *lived in Casper, Wyoming, between the ages of five and twelve. She currently lives in Burlington, Vermont, where she writes fiction and drama. Her plays have been produced in Indiana, Arizona, Missouri, Arkansas, and Vermont. Several of her plays and one of her adult stories are published in journals, including* Room of One's Own *and* Collages and Bricolages.

In the Autumn Grass

HAMLIN GARLAND

Did you ever lie low
In the depth of the plain,
In the lee of a swell that lifts
Like a low-lying island out of the sea,
    When the blue joint shakes
        As an army of spears;
    When each flashing wave breaks
    In turn overhead
        And wails in the door of your ears?

    If you have, you have heard
        In the midst of the roar,
    The note of a lone gray bird,
    Blown slantwise by overhead
    As he swiftly sped
        To his south-land haven once more!

O the music abroad in the air,
With the autumn wind sweeping
His hand on the grass, where
The tiniest blade is astir, keeping
Voice in the dim, wide choir,

Of the infinite song, the refrain,
The wild, sad wail of the plain!

A Pulitzer Prize-winning author, **Hamlin Garland** *was probably best known for his short stories and his memoir,* A Son of the Middle Border. *Born in 1860, he spent his childhood in Wisconsin, Iowa, and South Dakota. In addition to writing, Hamlin Garland worked as an advocate for better treatment of American Indians.*

Big Grass

LOUISE ERDRICH

*Although most of the tallgrass prairie has been plowed under for agricul-
ture, the grasses that define it persist in both protected and overlooked
places, which Louise Erdrich celebrates in this essay.*

My father loves the small and receding wild places in the
agribusiness moonscape of North Dakota cropland, and so do
I. Throughout my childhood, we hunted and gathered in the
sloughs, the sandhills, the brushy shelterbelts and unmowed
ditches, on the oxbows and along the banks of mudded rivers
of the Red River valley. On the west road that now leads to the
new Carmelite monastery just outside of Wahpeton, we picked
prairie rosehips in fall and dried them for vitamin C-rich teas
in the winter. There was always, in the margins of the cornfield
just beyond our yard, in the brushy scraps of abandoned pasture, right-of-ways along the railroad tracks, along the river itself, and in the corners and unseeded lots of the town, a lowly
assertion of grass.

It was big grass. Original prairie grass—bluestem and
Indian grass, side-oats grama. The green fringe gave me the
comforting assurance that all else planted and tended and set
down by humans was somehow temporary. Only grass is eternal. Grass is always waiting in the wings.

Before high-powered rifles and a general dumbing down of hunting attitudes, back when hunters were less well armed, and anxious more than anything to put meat on their tables, my father wore dull green and never blaze orange. He carried a green fiberglass bow with a waxed string, and strapped to his back a quiver of razor-tipped arrows. Predawn on a Saturday in fall he'd take a child or two into the woods near Hankinson, Stack Slough, or the cornfields and box elder and cottonwood scruff along the Wild Rice or Bois de Sioux rivers. Once, on a slim path surrounded by heavy scrub, my father and I heard a distant crack of a rifle shot and soon, crashing toward us, two does and a great gray buck floated. Their bounds carried them so swiftly that they nearly ran us over.

The deer huffed and changed direction midair. They were so close I felt the tang of their panic. My father didn't shoot—perhaps he fumbled for his bow but there wasn't time to aim—more likely, he decided not to kill an animal in front of me. Hunting was an excuse to become intimate with the woods and fields, and on that day, as on most, we came home with bags of wild plums, elmcap mushrooms, more rosehips.

Since my father began visiting the wild places in

the Red River valley, he has seen many of them destroyed. Tree cover of the margins of rivers, essential to slow spring runoff and the erosion of topsoil—cut and leveled for planting. Wetlands—drained for planting. Unplowed prairie (five thousand acres in a neighboring Minnesota county)—plowed and planted. From the air, the Great Plains is now a vast earth-toned Mondrian painting, all strict right angles of fields bounded by thin and careful shelterbelts. Only tiny remnants of the tallgrass remain. These pieces in odd cuts and lengths are like the hems of long and sweeping old-fashioned skirts. Taken up, the fabric is torn away, forgotten. And yet, when you come across the original cloth of grass, it is an unfaded and startling experience. Here is a reminder that before this land was a measured product tended by Steiger tractors with air-cooled cabs and hot-red combines, before this valley was wheat and sugar-beet and sunflower country, before the drill seeders and the windbreaks, the section measures and the homesteads, this was the northern tallgrass prairie.

It was a region mysterious for its apparent simplicity.

Grass and sky were two canvases into which rich details painted and destroyed themselves with joyous intensity. As sunlight erases cloud, so fire ate grass and restored grass in a cycle of unrelenting power. A prairie burned over one year blazes out, redeemed in the absolving mist of green the next. On a warm late-winter day, snow slipping down the sides of soft prairie rises, I can feel the grass underfoot collecting its bashful energy. Big bluestem, female and green sage, snakeweed, blue grama, ground cherry, Indian grass, wild onion, purple coneflower, and purple aster all spring to life on a prairie burned the previous year.

To appreciate grass, you must lie down in grass. . . . Just

after the snow has melted each spring, it is good to throw one-self on grass. The stems have packed down all winter, in swirls like a sleeper's hair. The grass sighs and crackles faintly, a weighted mat, releasing fine winter dust.

It is that smell of winter dust I love best, rising from the cracked stalk. Tenacious in its cycle, stubborn in its modest re-fusal to die, the grass embodies the philosopher's myth of eternal return. *All flesh is grass* is not a depressing conceit to me. To see ourselves within our span as creatures capable of quiet and continual renewal gets me through those times when the writing stinks, I've lost my temper, overloaded on wine choco-lates, or am simply lost to myself. Snow melts. Grass springs back. Here we are on a quiet rise, finding the first uncanny shoots of green.

My daughters' hair has a scent as undefinable as grass—made up of mood and weather, of curiosity and water. They part the stiff waves of grass, gaze into the sheltered universe. Just to be, just to exist—that is the talent of grass. Fire will pass over. The growth tips are safe underground. The bluestem's still the scorched bronze of late-summer deer pelts. Formaldehyde ants swarm from a warmed nest of black dirt. The ants seem electrified, driven, ridiculous in tiny self-importance. Watching the ants, we can delight in our lucky indolence. They'll follow one another and climb a stem of grass threaded into their nest to the end, until their weight bows it to the earth. There's a clump of crested wheatgrass, a foreigner, invading. The breast feather of a grouse. A low hunker of dried ground cherries. Sage. Still silver, its leaves specks and spindrels, sage is a gener-ous plant, releasing its penetrating scent of freedom long after it is dried and dead. And here, the first green of the year rises in the female sage, showing at the base in the tiny budded lips.

Horned larks spring across the breeze and there, off the rent ice, the first returning flock of Canada geese search out the open water of a local power plant on the Missouri River. In order to recreate as closely as possible the mixture of forces that groomed the subtle prairie, buffalo are included, at Cross Ranch Preserve, for grazing purposes. Along with fire, buffalo were the keepers of the grass and they are coming back now, perhaps because they always made sense. They are easier to raise than cattle, they calve on their own, and find winter shelter in brush and buffalo-berry gullies.

From my own experience of buffalo—a tiny herd lives in Wahpeton and I saw them growing up and still visit them now—I know that they'll eat most anything that grows on the ground. In captivity, though, they relish the rinds of watermelon. The buffalo waited for and seemed to know my parents, who came by every few days in summer with bicycle baskets full of watermelon rinds. The tongue of a buffalo is long, gray, and muscular, a passionate scoop. While they eat watermelon, the buffalo will consent to have their great boulder foreheads scratched but will occasionally, over nothing at all, or perhaps everything, ram themselves into their wire fences. I have been on the other side of a fence charged by a buffalo and I was stunned to a sudden blank-out at the violence.

One winter, in the middle of a great snow, the buffalo walked up and over their fence and wandered from their pen by the river. They took a route through the town. There were reports of people stepping from their trailers into the presence of shaggy monoliths. The buffalo walked through backyards, around garages, took the main thoroughfares at last into the swept-bare scrim of stubble in the vast fields—into their old range, after all.

Grass sings, grass whispers. Ashes to ashes, dust to grass. But real grass, not the stuff that we trim and poison to an acid green mat, not clipped grass never allowed to go to seed, not this humanly engineered lawn substance as synthetic as a carpet. Every city should have a grass park, devoted to grass, long grass, for city children haven't the sense of grass as anything but scarp on a boulevard. To come into the house with needlegrass sewing new seams in your clothes, the awns sharp and clever, is to understand botanical intelligence. Weaving through the toughest boots, through the densest coat, into the skin of sheep, needlegrass will seed itself deep in the eardrums of dogs and badgers. And there are other seeds, sharp and eager, diving through my socks, shorter barbs sewn forever into the laces and tongues of my walking boots.

Grass streams out in August, full grown to a hypnotizing silk. The ground begins to run beside the road in waves of green water. A motorist, distracted, pulls over and begins to weep. Grass is emotional, its message a visual music with rills and pauses so profound it is almost dangerous to watch. Tallgrass in motion is a world of legato. Returning from a powwow my daughter and I are slowed and then stopped by the spectacle and we drive side roads, walk old pasture, until we find real grass turned back silver, moving, running before the wind. Our eyes fill with it and on a swale of grass we sink down, chewing the ends of juicy stems.

Soon, so soon.

Your arms reach, dropping across the strings of an air harp. . . . You don't mind dying quite so much. You don't fear turning into grass. You almost believe that you could continue, from below, to express in its motion your own mesmeric yearning, and yet find cheerful comfort. For grass is a plant of homey endurance, pure fodder after all.

I would be converted to a religion of grass. *Sleep the winter away and rise headlong each spring. Sink deep roots. Conserve water. Respect and nourish your neighbors and never let trees gain the upper hand.* Such are the tenets and dogmas. As for the practice—*grow lush in order to be devoured or caressed, stiffen in sweet elegance, invent startling seeds*—those also make sense. *Bow beneath the arm of fire. Connect underground. Provide. Provide. Be lovely and do no harm.*

Louise Erdrich *is the author of several novels, including* The Beet Queen, Love Medicine, *and* The Antelope Wife. *She grew up in North Dakota and is of German-American and Turtle Mountain Ojibwa descent.*

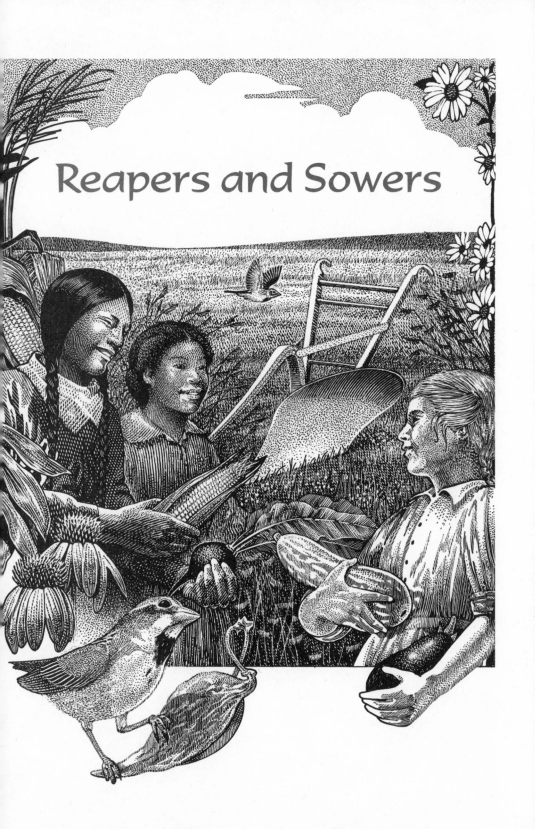

Reapers and Sowers

Going Home to Nicodemus

DANIEL CHU AND BILL SHAW

For many settlers, the prairie offered a chance for a new beginning and a better life. These opportunities were especially meaningful for one group of nineteenth-century Americans: African Americans who had just gained their freedom from slavery.

The year was 1878, and Willianna Hickman found herself in a place she had never been before. Kansas was its name, and it was, Willianna had been told, the "Promised Land."

Willianna Hickman was thirty-one years old and a woman of color. This was one of the terms commonly used in the nineteenth century to describe an African American. Willianna and her husband, the Reverend Daniel Hickman, had traveled to Kansas from Georgetown, in north-central Kentucky, where the Reverend Hickman had been the minister of the Mount Olive Baptist Church.

All but the youngest in Daniel's Kentucky congregation had been born in slavery. But now, thirteen years after the end of the American Civil War, they were free men and women. No longer could they be bought and sold as property to be kept or disposed of at the whim of masters.

For all that, however, America's leaders had not given enough thought as to what was to become of the four million freed slaves in the South. The freed men and women owned neither land nor homes and had little, if any, money. Most could not read or write. During slavery, they had toiled on southern plantations as field hands or household servants. They knew little else.

Now they were at liberty to leave the plantations and go wherever they wished. But where would that be? How were they to feed and house themselves? Where would they find work? How could people who had so little survive?

For the members of Reverend Hickman's church group, an answer came during the winter of 1877–1878. It came in the person of a white visitor named W. R. Hill.

W. R. Hill was a land promoter from Kansas, far away to the west. Hill told the Georgetown church members that there was government land available for homesteading on the western frontier. There was lots of it, and it was practically free for the asking. To claim a quarter section of land—160 acres—a homesteader had little more to do than show up.

Think of it! How could someone who had nothing, and no way of getting anything, turn down an offer like that?

The idea of homesteading became more attractive as Hill talked on. He and his partners had put together a special package for blacks only: a new town on the prairie run by blacks exclusively for blacks. Even as he spoke, W. R. Hill confided, hundreds of black settlers already were moving to this new community, a town that bore an intriguing name: Nicodemus.

To the Georgetown, Kentucky, church audience on that wintry night, W. R. Hill's words were like an answered prayer. Here was a chance, the first for any of them, to own a piece of land, to be independent and self-supporting, to make their own way in life. It was a chance to leave behind the racial hostility and discrimination they had always known.

Out on the open plains of the Kansas frontier, W. R. Hill said, blacks and whites would live as equals.

With the coming of spring, about two hundred members of the Reverend Hickman's church packed up their few belongings and joined the great western migration. From the hills of Kentucky, they went off in two groups for Kansas and a new life.

The migrants from Kentucky reached Ellis in western Kansas by rail in just a few days. But an outbreak of measles among the children brought sudden tragedy. Some of them died, but Daniel and Willianna Hickman and their six children were among the luckier ones. They survived the outbreak. After a two-week delay in Ellis, the Hickmans and the other families hired horses and wagons for the final leg of their journey.

What a journey it was!

Guided by compass, they traveled two more days across roadless plains marked here and there by a few trees, deer trails, and buffalo wallows, or watering holes. At night the men built roaring campfires and fired their guns in the air to keep wild animals away. The women unpacked bedding and cooked a meal while the children slept or played games within the shadow of the fire's glow.

Worn from travel, Willianna Hickman was almost totally spent by the time her group arrived at its destination. She felt even worse when she got her first look at it.

Nicodemus was not the Promised Land she had expected, not what she had hoped for. To Willianna's dismay, there lay before her an entire community of people living in holes in the ground. The people were burrowed into the earth like the prairie dogs Willianna had seen on the trek from Ellis.

More than half a century later, when she was ninety, Willianna Hickman still vividly remembered her shock and astonishment on that spring day in 1878:

> When we got in sight of Nicodemus, the men shouted, "There is Nicodemus." Being very sick, I hailed this news with gladness. I looked with all the eyes I had. "Where is Nicodemus? I don't see it." My husband pointed out various smokes coming out of the ground and said, "That is Nicodemus." The families [there] lived in dugouts. . . . . The scenery was not at all inviting, and I began to cry.
>
> —*Topeka (Kansas) Daily Capital,* 1937

❧

> My grandad and grandma got here in Nicodemus and stayed. They used to go from here to Ellis in wagons to get groceries. They'd stay there all night and come back the next morning. They said the wolves were real bad along the way. They'd have meat in the wagons, and they'd get up there and beat the wolves off, knocked 'em on the head with clubs and things.
>
> —Nicodemus farmer Don Moore, in a 1993 interview

Most of the first pioneers to arrive in Nicodemus came in five separate groups. The members of each group already knew one another, whether as relatives, friends, or members of the same church. And because they had bonded in some way beforehand and understood the need to pull together, they formed the solid core that saw Nicodemus through its first trying days and years.

W. R. Hill himself guided the first group of thirty settlers to the townsite on July 30, 1877. He brought them in from Topeka, the state capital 240 miles to the east, where the group had been organized by Hill, Roundtree, and Z. (Zach) T. Fletcher.

Jenny Fletcher, Zach's wife, was the only woman in Nicodemus during the first month. She and Zach's brother, T. (Thomas) J. Fletcher, would be bulwarks of strength when the going was the toughest.

It took no time at all for the first arrivals to realize that their Promised Land was not very promising. Many felt cheated and began to talk openly of hanging W. R. Hill.

Hill decided that his wisest move at that moment would be to hide. He sought out the home of a white friend for refuge. Later he was concealed in a wagon load of hay and smuggled to the town of Stockton twenty miles to the east. W. R. Hill stayed in Stockton until the anger in Nicodemus subsided.

In September 1877 a second group of 130 families, numbering about 300 people, reached Nicodemus, this time from Lexington, Kentucky. Many of them took one look at the empty prairie and were not happy with what they saw. The very next day, sixty of the families turned around and headed back east.

Those who did stay soon realized that they had come to Nicodemus too late in the growing season. There would be no harvest the first year. Their problem was compounded by the fact that the town promoters had not bought any supplies to tide the community over the first winter. And the nearest grocery store was at the railhead at Ellis, a walk of more than thirty miles each way.

But hadn't W. R. Hill told them that there was an abundance of wild game that could be hunted for food?

Yes, he had. But by this time, the game animals that might have been turned into meat for the table had migrated elsewhere in their own search for winter pasture.

With the onset of colder days and nights, shelter became a pressing need. At first the pioneers of Nicodemus huddled under makeshift lean-tos. But the relentless prairie winds blew the rickety structures to shreds.

Build cabins? The scarcity of timber made that impossible. Buy lumber? Even if they had the money—and most did not— there was not a commercial lumber mill close by.

So the Nicodemus pioneers did what they had to do. They burrowed into the ground. They built dugouts.

A dugout is just what it sounds like: a hole in the ground usually dug into the side of a small hill. Wielding hand tools such as picks, spades, or hoes, the dugout builders excavated a rectangular space maybe fifteen or so feet long, fourteen feet wide, and about six feet deep. Because the terrain was slightly sloped, a portion of the dugout remained above ground. That part was enclosed by "bricks" made from the prairie sod itself.

The method for roofing a dugout was to lay willow saplings, tree branches, and prairie brush across a long ridgepole. Then a layer of dirt was piled and packed on top.

Entry to the dugout was through a door at one end with steps leading down to the dirt floor. A fireplace and chimney took up most of the other end.

Dugouts were unpleasant to live in. They were as dark,

cramped, and stuffy as small caves. But they provided a shelter from the weather, and they could be built cheaply and quickly, especially if neighbors pitched in to help.

Which was exactly how the Nicodemus settlers built their first dugout. They had to hurry, for one of them, Mrs. Emily Williams, the wife of Charles Williams, was about to give birth.

Inside that dugout on October 30, 1877, Emily Williams gave birth to a son. Henry Williams was the first baby born in Nicodemus, Kansas.

Huddled in their dugouts, the Nicodemus settlers, including the infant, Henry Williams, endured that first winter. Sympathetic whites in nearby communities helped out with food. Help also came from Indians who were passing through.

These were the Osage Indians, a settled tribe in eastern Kansas, whose annual hunts took them into the Rocky Mountains. On their return trip, the Osage saw the plight of the Nicodemus pioneers. In the spirit of compassion and generosity that could often be found on the frontier, the Osage shared their meat supply with the hungry blacks.

The new Nicodemites soon absorbed the lessons of survival on the High Plains. Jackrabbits could be snared, for example, and turned into a main dish. Sunflower stalks, willow twigs, and even dried animal dung—called "chips," as in "buffalo chips"—could be collected and burned as fuel for cooking and heating.

The smoke rising out of the ground from their fires was what Willianna Hickman saw when the next wave of settlers reached Nicodemus the following spring.

Daniel Chu *has been an editor and writer at* People, Newsweek, *and* Scholastic *magazines. The author of three previous books for young readers, he lives in New York City.* **Bill Shaw** *is a journalist and writer who has contributed to* People, Life, *and many other magazines and newspapers. He lives in Westfield, Indiana.*

Raspberries

Georgia Cook

It's an antique knowledge, berrying.
My mother learned it from her mother,
and her mother from hers, and so on.
Leave the house alone:
kettle, worn shoes, trousers, man's shirt,
disappear into the fields,
be absent for hours.

Raspberries braid a mesh to discourage interlopers,
but if you move slowly, the nettles don't scratch.
Fruitful corners must be unraveled and
unraveled again after a rain.
Ripe ovaries will drop at touch into your kettle;
pink to white ones don't let go.
Check each berry for tiny beetles
that gorge on the purple flesh.

In the west corner of my backyard,
raspberries, with weedy persistence,
push up shaggy scouts late into September.
Fenced, old stalks cut back each fall,
I own a generous patch,
and when the city is spongy in July heat,

the resident jays and grackles scolding on overhead wires,
I harvest whistling sweetness,
pink frozen light.

Georgia Cook *is a single mother of three daughters, a public-school teacher, and a writer of poetry, young-adult novels, and family history. She currently lives in Minnesota.*

A Poppin' Tale

HELEN COLELLA

This story is adapted from a popular tall tale about Nebraska. While tall tales are known for their exaggeration, some say the peculiarities of the weather in this region cannot be overstated.

Anyone and everyone who has ever lived in or visited Nebraska knows all about the weather. It is, without a doubt, a topic of conversation in every town, on every farm, and with everybody.

"Weather 'round these parts is just plain curious," says the mayor.

"Unusual. Unmanageable. Unpredictable," says the mayor's wife.

At the town hall, the local grocery store, or the school, you can hear tell of how familiar folks are with Mother Nature's sense of humor.

Hot. Cold. Wet. Dry. Windy. Calm. The weather is indeed unusual, unmanageable, unpredictable, and unavoidable.

"Gets so hot," says one lady, "that sometimes I don't even have to cook breakfast. The hens on our farm lay fried eggs."

"Gets so cold," says another, "that the icicles hanging down off the roof come inside to get warm."

"Gets so wet," says one young boy, "that the ducks swimming in the pond have to use umbrellas."

"Gets so dry," says one farmer, "that the cows give powdered milk."

"Gets so windy," says another, "that it shears the sheep and rolls the wool into skeins."

"Gets so calm," says one young girl, "that you can hear the wheat snoring in the fields."

Nebraskans also know that without any warning the weather can change. It can come and go before you finish sayin' your own name.

On one particular hot, lazy day in August, the weather took a strange turn. The sky filled with dark rain clouds. Thunder roared. Rain fell in torrents. It soaked the land for miles and miles. It changed ponds into lakes and streams into rivers. And the rivers themselves reached worrisome levels.

"Like walkin' on a sponge," recalls one man.

"Sure enough," says another. "Folks worried about their farmland washing away."

This storm came up fast and furious. Took everyone by surprise. Outdid anything that had ever passed through these parts before.

For miles and miles, straight ahead, you could see nothing but rain. But what was unusual about all this was that the stormin' only disturbed half the land. The other half sat right next to it soakin' in the hot, blazin' sun.

"Never saw anything like it," says one lady.

The legend tells about one farmer who came into some good fortune. Not because he did anything different from the other farmers, but rather from pure good luck.

Seems that the old farmer had planted his crops in just the right place. His sugar beet, up on a hill. His corn, down in the valley below.

Now on this day, two things happened. The rain drenched the beets. Gave them the bath of a lifetime. The sun, hotter than it had ever been, cooked the corn, right on the cob. Kernels started a-poppin'.

As if that weren't enough weather to talk about, up came the wind. Put in its two cents. It whipped that rain against the sugar beets. Washed all the juice from their inners down the hill. What a sticky mess! It gushed at top speed. It pushed and rolled the popped corn, turning it into cornballs.

"Of utmost size," says the farmer.

No sooner had all this stormin' stopped when the local gossips got to talkin'. Word spread fast: "Giant-sized cornballs are taking over the farmland."

At first the farmer who owned the land couldn't believe what the fuss was all about. But when looky-loos from every county around came to see, some carrying forks and knives, he got a great idea.

He set up a stand at the edge of his farm, with a big red sign that said: MOTHER NATURE'S NATURAL CORNBALL TREATS. FIFTY CENTS A TASTE.

"An enterprising idea, if I say so myself," he says.

No one knows for sure whether or not the weather really passed in this fashion. No one knows for sure if the farmer became rich and famous. But if you talk to anyone from Nebraska, they'll probably tell you about the best tastin' cornballs ever.

Grandma's Caramel Cornballs

Ingredients:

    1 cup popcorn (unpopped)
    1 cup butter or margarine

½ cup corn syrup

2 cups brown sugar

¼ teaspoon cream of tartar

1 teaspoon salt

½ teaspoon baking soda

1 teaspoon burnt sugar (heat sugar in a small
saucepan until it turns into a dark
brown liquid)

Preparation:

Pop the corn. Set it aside.

Combine butter, corn syrup, and brown sugar in a sauce-pan. Boil for 5 minutes. Remove from heat.

Add the remaining ingredients in the listed order. This is the caramel.

Pour the caramel over the popcorn. Stir well to coat each piece.

While the mixture is warm and sticky, scoop up a handful. Shape the caramel corn into balls. (Be careful here; the caramel mixture may be hot.)

Place in a shallow baking pan. Bake in the oven at 200 degrees Fahrenheit for an hour. Stir occasionally.

Enjoy!

~⌣~

Wife and mother of four, **Helen Colella** *has written stories for adults and children, coauthored two teacher's guides and four geography workbooks, and written her own history activity book. She works as an editor and writer for* Art Revue Magazine *in Loveland, Colorado.*

Recollections

IRON TEETH

Iron Teeth was ninety-two years old and living on the Tongue River Reservation in eastern Montana when she told her life story to Dr. Thomas B. Marquis, the agency doctor, in 1926. This excerpt is drawn from that interview, which was published in Marquis's book, The Cheyennes of Montana.

Ninety-two years ago I was born in the Black Hills country. The time of my birth was in the moon when the berries are ripe, in the last part of the summer. My father was a Cheyenne Indian, my mother was a Sioux. My parents brought up their family as members of the Cheyenne tribe. Our people traveled over the whole country between the Elk River and Mexico. . . .

My grandmother told me that when she was young our people did not have any horses. When they needed to go anywhere they put their packs upon dogs or on little pole travois drawn by dogs. The people themselves had to walk. In those times they did not travel far nor often. But when they got horses they could move more easily from place to place. Then they could kill more of the buffalo and other animals, and so they got more meat for food and gathered more skins for lodges and clothing.

I remember when parties of our men used to go afoot from

the Black Hills far southward to get horses. Each man took along only his lariat rope, his bow and arrows, his sheath-knife, a little package of dried meat, and two or three extra pairs of moccasins tucked into his belt. Their women were sad in heart as they made these moccasins, for sometimes the travelers were gone a whole year, or sometimes they were killed. . . .

We planted corn every year when I was a little girl in the Black Hills. With sharpened sticks we punched holes in the ground, dropped in the grains of corn, then went hunting all summer. When the grass died we returned and gathered the crop. But the Pawnees and the Arikaras got to stealing or destroying our growing food, so we had to quit the plantings. We got into the way then of following all the time after the buffalo and other game herds.

We learned of vegetable foods growing wild. We gathered wild turnips, wild sweet potatoes, and other root foods. We found out the best place for berries. One time, when we were traveling past some white settlements, our people got a few watermelons. These were to us a new kind of food. The women cut them up and put them into pots for boiling. After a while they looked into the pots and found nothing but water and seeds.

Our dolls were made by tying a stuffed buckskin head on the end of a forked stick. Such a doll had hair glued to the head, beads for eyes, and a face painted on the buckskin. The stuffing for the head was buffalo hair. The clothing was of beaded and fringed buckskin. We girls built playhouse tepees for ourselves and our dolls. We would hang little pieces of meat out upon bushes and play like we were drying meat, the same as our mothers did at the home lodges. Sometimes we would play at moving camp. The boys would come with willow baskets.

Everything would be put into the baskets and then the boys would drag them to wherever we might want to go. We would ride stick horses. The doll might ride on a stick horse beside the play-mother, or it might be carried on her back.

My mother made me a fine doll that I kept in a rawhide satchel with its extra clothing and moccasins. But I lost it. The Pawnees came and attacked our camp. All of the women and children went running, without stopping to take anything from the lodges. I had to leave my satchel and the doll behind. For a long time afterward, many times I cried over that lost baby. At night I dreamed about the enemy having scalped it and cut up its body.

A great issue of government presents was made to the Cheyennes when I was 15 years old. The place was near the forks of what we called Horse River and Geese River. Soldier houses had just been built there. We were given beef, but we did not care for this kind of meat. Great piles of bacon were stacked upon the prairie and distributed to us, but we used it only to make fires or to grease robes for tanning. We got soda but did not know what to do with it. Green coffee was distributed among us. We supposed the grains were some new kind of berries. We boiled them as they were, green, but they did not taste good. We liked the sugar presented to us. They gave us plenty of it, some of it light brown and some dark brown.

We got brass kettles, coffeepots, curve-bladed butcher knives and sharp-pointed sewing awls, which were better than ours that were made of bone. There were boxfuls of black and white thread for us. The thread was in skeins, not on spools. All of the women got black goods, colored goods and bed-ticking material. We made the cloth into summer clothing for children and draperies for the interiors of the lodges. We were given plenty of colored beads, brass buttons, brass finger rings, and red and blue face paints. Blankets were issued out to everybody. None of them had mixed colors. All were of some one or other solid color—red, blue, yellow, green, white. No shawls were given. It was some time afterward when we first saw shoulder shawls. Also, it was some time afterward when we first saw blankets having mixed colors. I first saw them among the Crows.

Our chief told us: "These presents are given to us because the white people are friendly and they want us to become civilized, as they are." Two certain white men did most of the gift distributing at this time. We called one of them Yellow White Man. He belonged with the Crow Indians. The other was a full white man. He gave us the blankets, so we called him Blanket White Man, or Blanket. The Cheyennes knew him after that time. We learned the white people called him Jim Bridger.

The first time I rode alone on horseback occurred when I was about ten years old. My father gave me a yearling colt. When we were traveling, my mother would put packs upon the colt with me. Usually I had two badger skins filled with dried chokecherries behind me, swinging down the colt's sides. Boys teased me by riding up close and lashing my colt to make it jump. At first I was frightened and they laughed at me. But I soon got used to it, and after a little while I became a good rider.

After I grew older I liked to break horses. When I became a woman I never asked any man to tame my horses for me. Before trying to ride them, my sister and I used to take the wild animals to a sandy place beside the river. Sometimes we would lead one out into deep water before mounting it. A horse cannot buck hard in deep water. One time a bucking horse threw me into a deep and narrow ditch, where I lit upon my back. My sister had to help me out from the ditch, but I was not hurt. I was never badly hurt in this way nor any other way. I never had a broken bone. I have been shot at many times but no bullet or arrow ever hit me.

Lots of wild horses used to be running loose on the plains to the southward. I had a good running horse when I was a young woman, and I always carried with me a lariat rope made of spun and plaited buffalo hair. As a girl I played a romping game we called "wild horses," in which some children would run here and there while others would try to throw lariats about their bodies. In this way I learned to toss the rope. One time, after my marriage, I was riding with my baby strapped to my back when I saw some wild horses. I put the baby in its cradle board down on the prairie and got after the herd. That day I caught two horses.

I was married to Red Ripe when I was 21 years old. But my name was not changed. The Indian women of the old times did not lose their own names on account of marriage. In my girlhood I was called *Mah-i-ti-wo-nee-ni*—Iron Teeth. All through my life I have been known to my people by this same name.

—◆—

Iron Teeth *spent her early years living on the northern plains before her family was relocated to Indian Territory in Oklahoma. In 1878, she and her family escaped the reservation. They managed to reach Nebraska, only to be imprisoned by the U.S. Army. When they attempted another escape, many in the group were killed, including Iron Teeth's oldest son. Iron Teeth and other survivors were eventually recaptured and sent to live on the Tongue River Reservation in Montana, where she lived for the rest of her life.*

Two Strangers Come to Maggie's Prairie

CAROL GREEN

This story is based on the life of a real North Dakota girl named Mabel Bergeson, or Maggie. During World War I Maggie and her family lived on a farm near Streeter, North Dakota. Though far from the action, they were not beyond the war's reach.

Maggie pulled at the tall bluestem grass with its three blades on top that made it look like a turkey's foot. She dangled it in her mouth. Mama's low voice, singing a Swedish folk tune, came from the milk shed. She and Annie, Maggie's older sister, were cleaning the more than two hundred parts of the separator. Maggie watched a red-tailed hawk soar high in the sky, glad she could be outside in the North Dakota prairie she loved. She hated being cooped up inside doing household chores.

King whinnied and Maggie answered back with a low whinnying sound. "Can't play this morning. The haying won't wait." She turned toward the north forty thinking, Soon, King, you'll be old enough to ride. She remembered that first morning and the death of the mare, his mama. King was so frightened. Now, though, he was almost a full-grown stallion with fine Morgan blood.

Maggie hurried the last steps to the mower. Papa already

had Fanny and Prince hitched up. They snorted eagerly in the still morning air. Papa nodded but didn't say a word.

She climbed up and easily threw the lever that lowered the six-foot-long blade from its vertical position to its horizontal one. Despite being only ten, she could arm wrestle farm boys one or two years older than she. But she never told Mama that she always won. Mama hated Maggie's having to work so hard and their not being able to afford a hired hand.

Maggie watched Papa walk to where Bergie and Emma, the twins, waited to rake the field she mowed yesterday. Lucky them, Maggie thought, they can work together. And anyway, they're only eight. Papa doesn't make them work as hard or as long as me. Maggie knew that all morning and afternoon her only company, besides the horses' foot stompings and tail swishings, would be the sliding whistle sounds of the meadowlark.

She clucked to the horses. The mower's scissorlike blade set to work. She loved watching the hay topple over. Each forward step of the horses made the hay ripple like a yellow-green wave. Soon a wide path stretched for what seemed like miles across the prairie. Maggie thought, I did it. I made it happen.

She squinted back toward the house, which gleamed white in the sunshine. Even the roof seemed silvered bright. Next to the house a most beautiful pond seemed to wait. A pond of pinks and reds made from the tiny blossoms of the wild prairie rose, Mama's favorite. Maggie could almost smell their luscious fragrance. Not a tree, not another house, came into view.

She yanked off her bonnet, hoping for the slightest breeze. But only pesky gnats flew around her sweaty face. She turned toward the edge of the slough. Dragonflies with their silver wings magically lifted up, then down. Their long bodies glistened blue-green in the hot sunlight. She stretched her arms, then sank down. Fanny gave a snort. "Hold on there, Fanny. Almost done. One more row."

Annie's voice broke into her thoughts. "M-A-G-G-I-E!" Quickly Maggie scrambled down and unhitched the horses. She slapped their rumps and watched them head for the pasture and a cool drink from the watering trough.

Halfway back to the house, Emma grabbed Maggie's arm. "Come on." She pulled Maggie toward the field of blue flax. "Let's go for a swim." Maggie got the giggles and ran ahead of Emma. The field of flax stretched bluer than any ocean or brighter than any summer sky.

She lifted up her foot as if pretending to test the water. Then, in one motion, she kneeled and lay flat on her stomach. With her arms she pretended to be swimming.

Emma sank in beside her, giggling. "Our very own ocean of blue flowers." She stopped. "What if Papa sees the flattened parts?"

"He won't," Maggie said, standing. "There's acres of blue." She touched the small blue flowers, letting them trickle across her fingers like droplets of water. "Come on. Lunch is waiting." She put her finger to her lips. "Don't tell."

That afternoon Maggie got the mail as always. She rushed to the house out of breath. Waving the envelope, she shouted, "Mama, Mama. It's the war department for Papa."

Without a word Mama took the letter and walked to the front room. Putting the envelope on Papa's desk, she said, "Best wait till after supper."

Maggie moaned, "After supper?" But Mama's sharp look told her enough. Maggie knew she wasn't to mention it to Annie, Emma—not anyone.

At supper Maggie somehow managed to force down the steaming hot stew, barely tasting it. All she wanted was for Papa to pick up his coffee and head for the front room, like always. Instead, he walked out on the porch. Maggie clenched her fist. How can I get him to go into the front room?

She followed Papa outside and stared up at the sky. The early morning rain clouds had vanished, leaving the air smelling squeaky clean like after your hair is washed. "Hans." Maggie jumped at Mama's one word. Mama handed Papa the letter. Its black bold letters—THE WAR DEPARTMENT—seemed bigger to Maggie than before. As Papa read, a heavy silence hung over them.

Finally, Papa looked up in disbelief. He nodded slowly, looking at Mama. Her fingers fumbled for her apron, then silent tears ran down her cheeks. Maggie's heart slammed against her chest. Tears, too, streamed from her eyes.

Mama's voice came out all uneven, but her tears had stopped. "If you go to war, I . . . I can't run the farm alone. What are we to do?"

Annie sobbed out, "Go to war?"

Bergie and Emma repeated, "War?" and burst into tears.

Papa stared off to the very edge of the prairie. Night's darkness had begun to crowd out most of the setting sun. Slowly he said, "I'll send a letter. There must be some mistake. They can't be drafting farmers." Mama nodded. Maggie nodded. And Papa headed for the front room.

Maggie followed Emma upstairs. No one said a word as they got ready for bed. Maggie couldn't even pray as she lay with her head on her pillow. She told herself, I won't think about war. Papa's letter will make it be all right.

The next day and the next and the next Maggie was glad for

the farm work and not having to go to school. She kept her silent worry inside her, not talking to even Mama.

Only her horse, King, knew her worry. He was her best friend. As she brushed his shiny coat, the words spilled out. "War. Teacher says it won't come to the farmland. It's far, far away." She brushed harder and harder. With each stroke, she felt her worries slip away. Standing a little taller, she hurried off to finish the mowing.

The next afternoon Maggie climbed up on the metal seat. She gently brushed a ladybug from her pant leg and watched its tiny wings lift as it flew off. Don't ladybugs mean good luck? They can't make Papa go to war. They just can't.

Without warning, her friend Lydia's father came to mind. She wondered, Would they draft him? He's a blacksmith, not a farmer. Maggie clucked to the horses—Birdie and Dick, a fresh team. An uneasiness filled her. Mr. Hoffer was German. Is it wrong to be German? It can't be, she decided. This is America.

"War." Maggie slapped the reins across Birdie's and Dick's backs. They gave a startled jump, then did their usual cross step into a turn. She prayed that there would not be any rocks. If a rock flies up, she thought, Birdie might bolt and drag us all to the barn. One more turn and this field will be done.

She pulled off her bonnet and brushed the sleeve of her arm across her forehead. The long hot days were good for growing, but now they seemed to inch by slower than the turn of the plow's iron wheels. It had been a week, yet Papa still hadn't received a reply from the war department.

On the last stretch Maggie heard the whinny of a horse. It wasn't King. She turned, spotting a buggy, one she had never seen before. No neighbor would be coming to call in the heat of the afternoon.

She jumped down and quickly tethered Birdie and Dick. Whistling for King, she inched just close enough to hear. The porch door slammed. Mama and Annie came out. Bergie and Emma stood next to her but didn't say a word. "Steady," Maggie said to King, feeling her own heart pounding in her ears.

Two men in military uniforms climbed out. They walked over to Papa and stiffly held out their hands. Just as stiffly, Papa nodded and shook their hands.

"Think they'll draft Papa?" Bergie asked, kicking a rock. Maggie shrugged, not trusting her own voice.

"These all your children?" the uniformed man on the left asked, pushing out the word "all."

Papa just nodded.

The other man asked, "No one else but you to run the farm?"

"Can't afford to hire someone. And no one to be had."

"How many acres?"

"Six hundred forty."

The man let out a low whistle.

"Tell you what," the taller of the two men said, "we'll see that you stay on the farm to grow the grain. We need it for the bread to feed our fighting boys."

Maggie felt a flood of relief. She stroked King's neck over and over. Suddenly she stiffened. The men weren't leaving. They were going into the barn. She put her arms around King. Then she heard the whinny of the dapplegrays. Holding fast to King, she whispered, "They can't take you. You're not full grown."

Coming out, the shorter man said, "You've got some mighty fine horse flesh, Mr. Bergeson."

As the other man walked with Papa and helped him tie the two dapplegrays to the back of the buggy, Papa said, "I'm honored to help out in any way I can." His words sounded proud, even excited.

Maggie gasped. Not the dapplegrays. They were Papa's favorites.

Then the taller man said, "We'll beat those Germans before you know it." He practically spit out the words, "those Germans." Maggie felt as if she'd been hit in the stomach. She'd never heard words spoken in that tone, so filled with hate. What did he mean, "those Germans?" Didn't he know

Lydia was her best friend? Without moving, she watched the buggy go down their lane until it was only a speck. The dapple-grays, their high-stepping prance, the war—Maggie's mind was a jumble of questions.

"You going to stand there staring until it's dark?" Bergie asked.

Disgusted, Maggie turned on her heel. He doesn't even care. Slowly she took in a deep breath. The fresh smell of the prairie flooded over her. The war couldn't come to North Dakota, could it?

Suddenly her feet were running as a flash of lightning streaked across the sky. She counted, then thunder filled the air. "Dick, Birdie," she panted. "I have to get them back safe to the barn, away from the metal mower." Quickly she unharnessed the straps and climbed up on Birdie's back. She clucked, urging both into a fast walk.

Dark rumbling clouds blanketed the sky. Rain poured down. Maggie loved the coolness of the rain, but each time lightning flashed a shiver went up her spine. "We're almost there," she told herself, whistling for King. He stood bravely facing the storm as if to show he wasn't afraid. But at her whistle, he followed her into the barn.

Papa put on Birdie's halter, then he and Maggie ran for the house. Maggie raced upstairs to get into dry clothes. She didn't want to see Papa's eyes, to see how hard it was for him to give up the dapplegrays. Unexpectedly, a strange pride came over her. She knew Papa had done the right thing. Now, if only the war could hurry and be over. She remembered the ladybug. She just knew the dapplegrays would be back.

Carol Green *graduated from Northwestern University with a degree in education. Now, with the loss of her eyesight, she uses a talking computer, "George," to write children's books, poems, and devotionals. She teaches writing workshops and performs dramatizations and storytelling.*

cornfields thaw out

ALURISTA

cornfields thaw out
    belted cross the land as
midwestern thunderclad clouds hover
       in omaha, the meat-packing houses
pack mexicans—mojo's what they call us
    while warm tortillas
       shake off the cold at noon
    down dodge st., down way down Q st.
           into the southside salsa
mornings boil dew
        and the stench of slaughtered beasts
    engulfs the nostrils
    and the thought of carnage prevails
nothing much is different in this barrio
    big foot and bigotry squatted
since then no buffalo hooftracks can be stalked
      even pheasants are weary
      of cowboys plucking feathers
      to adorn their stetson tops
and rabbits dread the wheel
      more than their ancient foe
    coyotes howl and german shepherds bark

the moonfull spring is
here, for a while only
for a short, short while
trees will bloom

Alurista *is a poet, lecturer, and novelist, whose books include* flori-
canto en aztlán *and* nationchild plumaroja. *He helped found the
first Xicano Studies department at San Diego State University.*

Disappearances

JULENE BAIR

*Small family farms are becoming less and less common in the prairie re-
gion. In this essay, Julene Bair tells us about her family, their Kansas
farm, and some of the changing ways of rural life.*

I grew up on the mild-green, short-tufted, buffalo grass
prairies of northwestern Kansas. The High Plains they are
called, and my family's spot upon them was Highland Farm.
We were lifted up on that great plain, four thousand feet above
sea level, exposed to the sky, not cradled and protected by the
earth the way Iowa or Minnesota farm families are. Each family in rural Kansas was alone together on the flat. At night we
had only distant yellow lights to remind us that we did have
neighbors. When those blinked off at bedtime, we were left
with the stars, which my dad said went on and on. Coyotes
howled in our front yard.

When the Thanksgiving season approaches, I think of that
home place and our big corner of Kansas more intensely than
at other times, though, to tell the truth, it is on my mind always. Our rock-hard farmyard, gnarly with implement tracks
and bony bumps, is the ground I walk on still, the given against
which the baseline of my city life is too many eons removed.

Thanksgiving, that day when we feasted on the bounty of

our work, was often a forlorn holiday in Kansas. The hour at the table was joyous, but the season itself boded emptiness and decline. This was especially true when we traveled on Thanksgiving day. I have visions of desolate blacktops, straight and narrow between flat fields of stubble. The destinations were ragged towns where widowed great-aunts lived, their nondescript Plymouths parked in the unpaved drives of their trailer houses. Wandering the foreign burg with a remote cousin, I would try to imagine glamour in the unfamiliar surroundings despite streets of inelegant frozen mud. The movie theater, if there was one, would be shuttered, and the only traffic would be a sedate dirty pickup, jiggling slowly over the ruts as a farmer, fed up with food and with his relatives, headed out to a pasture to check his livestock.

The high point of those Thanksgivings came for me once when my brother Clark, home from college in the far off, eastern part of the state, let me drive his black Pontiac GTO the entire hundred miles from our farm to Aunt Rosie's. I aimed the car with earnest precision, filling with pride as Clark complimented me. "Wow! You're a natural!"

Clark had graduated high school when I was only nine. He came home less and less frequently as the years passed, his departure merely the first of many disappearances I would witness. Thirty years later, he would be killed in a bicycling accident on Highway 1, in California. "So far afield," I wrote in a memorial piece a year or so after the funeral.

Thanksgivings at home were much better, although the guests delayed their arrival to the last anguished minute. Impatient, I would flee out into the frost-killed forest of my mother's yard. I bounced a stick along the sidewalk, stooped to cuddle a cat or dog, or went down to the barn to stroke the neck of Queenie, my ill-tempered mare. Sparks and dust would shoot up from her roan coat, thick for winter, causing her to lay her ears back and turn her rump on me. I would wander out to the back lot near the windbreak and climb around on ancient combines and in rusted truck cabs until finally I heard cars pulling into the yard.

The day was transformed. My girl cousins and I would dart back and forth among our aunts and uncles, swiping all the olives and sweet pickles off the relish tray. After the meal, we would tiptoe behind the barn and slide the door shut before Queenie made a dash for it. I would jam the cold bit into her mouth, then lead her out the front door and over to the abandoned concrete stock tank, where each cousin would perch in turn. After many attempts, we usually managed to get Queenie positioned right and steadied long enough for all to get aboard. We would ride out beyond the windbreak. Once, when a pheasant squawked and burst from the stubble, Queenie saw her chance and shied. My cousins and I, still holding on to one another, flew off. I clung to the reins, which jerked us around in an arc and thudded us to the ground beneath the mare's front feet. Bruised in that exploit, we all four grabbed shovels and went to work on the anthill out by the storm cellar. We dug out of scientific interest in hibernation, we explained to our parents, but really it was out of a will to wreak vengeance on the animal kingdom, no matter how far down the ladder we had to stoop.

I was drunk with companionship on those rare Thanksgiving afternoons. But dark would fall inevitably and the cousins would leave. The next morning the long weekend would begin. A thousand ewes chomped ensilage in the corrals, but the place seemed empty to me.

Our way of life was dying. I sensed this even then. Only old people lived in the fifty houses in my great-aunts' towns. Nearer home, a crop of widows and divorcees—my parents' sisters—began migrating, with my cousins, to Colorado cities. Eventually my brothers and I would follow, until today only my father and one of his sisters still own farms. No one in my generation works the land. Some of us have tried our hands at farming, but generally only when other options have fallen through. I, for instance, went back to the farm at thirty-five, pregnant and broke after a failed marriage. The return was humiliating, but soon the Kansas elements reclaimed me. Having been reared in the harsh environment, I hadn't felt truly alive since I last battled dirt and wind. That spring, I rejoiced in the texture of the earth behind the plow. In the shop, armed with a grease gun, I scooted on a dolly beneath tractors, soothed by the smell of dust and grease and by the massive machinery.

I reveled in the power of big farm equipment. Ancestors only a couple generations before me had made their tenuous claim on the prairie, and now we were thundering over it in tractors bigger than their houses. But I was greeted also with the old sense of decline. My parents, like so many farmers, had moved to town many years before, trading the farm I had grown up on for some ground closer to their other holdings. Children had spilled out of my grandparents' sod shanties, and I was living alone in a two-story, four-bedroom house with one baby boy. Dad commuted to this farm as if it were a factory, the land suited only for the mass production of crops, no longer a place to live.

The prairie of my childhood, with its cloud-shadowed rises and mild ravines, had disappeared. Instead of buffalo grass, rows of irrigated corn and soybeans veed into the distance. The state's floral pride, the sunflower, wasn't prominent along roadsides anymore, where only the toughest grasses survived the many poisons. When I walked through ditches on my way from the pickup to a waiting tractor, no grasshoppers clacked aloft to startle me. As a child, I had grown oblivious to their landings on my breastbone. The snake population had diminished as well, making such treks across ditches less foolhardy, but I missed the edge of adventure in the landscape.

Denuded of snakes and cousins, and of friends, life in Kansas was even lonelier than in my childhood. After two years, I began to make plans for my second migration.

Today, I live eight hundred miles away from western Kansas, too far to travel for brief holiday breaks, but I've returned the past four summers. I want my son to know his grandparents and their land. I cannot uproot myself completely, nor reconcile myself to the fact that this land, once lost, then briefly reclaimed, is not our future.

Summers are always a busy time in Kansas, as long as hail or drought hasn't laid waste to the crops. Wheat trucks barrel down the gravel roads in July, hauling their bounty to the elevators, then, rattling empty, career back to the fields, where the combines graze like giant mantises. I like to see the wheat before the machines pull in, a county full of it. I like to walk in it when it is unscathed and trackless, its trillions of bristles whispering.

It was on a day like that a couple summers ago, when the buds were burnished gold but the stalks still too green to cut, that I decided to pay a visit to the home place. The road carried me out there, past both abandoned and still vital farmsteads, where green combines and red trucks waited silent and ready, the sun glinting off their windshields. On the sole curve, past the Rickards' place, I felt the excitement in my belly from when I was a kid driving home from high school and would take it too fast. I drove with my windows down, the air rushing in, fire-lapped and dry. Fifteen miles of that, the tires rumbling over gravel, an occasional rock dinging the tail pipe, and then there it was, still five miles away but prominently visible because of the gentle rise on which it stood.

I parked below the knoll leading up to the house. Opening the car door onto what I expected to be mere heat and wind, I was startled by a deer with a huge crest of antlers. It tore out of the thicket that had once been our north yard, where Dad had braced up the cherry tree with a makeshift post-and-rail crutch, and leapt past the remnants of the sheep barn into the wheat field. The pasture beyond that long building had once seemed to reach into eternity but was now reduced to a single circle of wheat beneath the breadth of a pivot sprinkler. I watched the deer bound through the wheat like a merry-go-round animal, his rack aligned in the crosshairs of the vacant afternoon, then turned back to the house yard.

Some of my mother's yellow rose bushes were in bloom, and I imagined her posing before them, as she had for one of the pictures in the family photo album, the skirt of her house-dress hugging her belly and thighs in the wind, which was always too intense and bothersome—full of dust in summer and needling cold in winter—to be called a breeze. I walked carefully, pulling back the branches that had overgrown the sidewalk, trying not to break or trample anything that would make the deer's haven less familiar when he returned. Millions of moments circled inside me, stirred by this visit as were the leaves overhead, tossed by the perennial wind. Should I tell Mom about the deer and the flowers, I wondered? She would be pleased to hear about them, but reminding her of the empty house would upset her. She never would have agreed to the trade, she once told me, had she known the farmstead her father built would wind up abandoned.

Grand by local standards, the old house is a monument to our dead: Grandpa Carlson, with his bald head, his Swedish accent, and his way of turning big dreams into reality; Grandma Carlson, with her nubbin bun, her sternness, and her complaining; Uncle John, the farming hope of my mother's family, who was struck by lightning while driving a tractor; and now Clark, my older brother, who had died just the previous year. It was his death, so recent, that brought me to the home place that day.

Someone planted two evergreen trees after we moved. I had to lift their branches to make my way up the wide steps of the south porch. I ran my hand down the beveled glass in the front entry, then discovered the door unlocked. The house was as cold as a walk-in meat locker, holding the chill from the night. Glass still lined the sashes of the bay windows, some of it original, rippled, handblown—a wonder, since the Carlsons, then the Bairs, had raised children in the house, and at least two other families had lived in it since we left. I had forgotten how big the windows were. No easy chairs beckoned from in front of them, however, and the air conditioner had been removed from below the middle window, leaving a hole that framed a square patch of brush.

Upstairs, the hallway was still fifteen feet wide. Mom and Dad's room, gaping and bedless, still seemed mysterious, darker than the rest of the house, somehow taboo. The tiny room belonging to Bruce, the younger of my two brothers, looked over the backyard, which was a tangle of vines and Russian olive trees even when we were children. Had his vivid imagination stemmed from that disorder, from watching the pink flames of sunset through the branches? I lingered in Clark's room. He stared out at the same baked gray farmyard as I had, with its kochia weeds around the foundation of the barn and the dead cottonwood tree by the cracked concrete stock tank where my cousins and I had mounted Queenie, and he had been the first of our immediate family to migrate.

It seemed fitting, on this tour of the past, to save my room for last. Vacant like the others, it had been painted a rude aqua, though pink and blue ribbony things still swirled against a white background in the wallpapered closet. The only child with two windows, I had the influence of Clark's bleak easterly view as well as the romance of Mom's south yard, where her best irises grew and where the locust tree brushed the rails of the balcony. There had been a mocking-bird who clacked angrily at us whenever we ran up and down the rickety planks. Out that window I had first heard coyotes yelp, up close.

We took life in the house our grandfather built for granted. Like most kids, we fought and didn't know we loved each other and felt sorry for ourselves and longed to escape, but our lives had a spiritual edge. The sky, whether endless blue or roiling with thunderheads, dwarfed our vanity. At night, in the summer, Mom and Dad steadied us, each in turn as we reached the age for clinging to the front fence, our toes wedged in the wire. They told us in amazed tones what little they knew about the stars. Once we saw moving lights in the sky that no one could explain.

Now, staring at the miles of wheat where the immense fan of buffalo grass had once opened onto sky, I reflected on how ironic it was that our migration to the cities had not diminished our impact on the land. With the aid of machinery and chemicals, and with families a tenth of their former size, we conquered the Plains, not just out of greed, but out of a failure to recognize what we loved and that love was reason enough not to destroy. Unable to fill the Plains with people, we settled for writing our name onto every inch of them, lest we forget ourselves and succumb to the spiritual vastness. Our farm once seemed infinite and painfully empty, whereas today even the world has limits. Were I to visit the house at night, I could now track dozens of satellites in the sky overhead. With this technology, we photograph the globe whole, the daytime shots optimistic with blue oceans, green prairies, a swirl of delicate clouds. But night shots reveal the glitter of man-made lights, blue-white fire along seacoasts encroaching inland—my aunts, my cousins, my brothers, and I folding back on ourselves, devouring.

I went outside and leaned on the gate post of the south yard, facing into the wind and the billowing wheat. Two kingbirds dove and chattered at me, their bellies yellow as sunflower petals. Most likely, they were direct descendants of the pair who had nested in the locust during my childhood. I scanned the branches overhead. My whole life, it had been this tree I imagined whenever I heard "Rock-a-Bye Baby"—*Rock-a-bye baby, up in the treetop. When the wind blows, the cradle will rock. When the bough breaks. . . .* It had been this tree I thought of when Clark died. I had imagined a giant portion of it severed, as if by lightning. But the tree was thriving. The wind still gushed in its leaves. Its flat pods still rattled. On the outer reaches of a southern branch a nest bobbed, framed in blue. Fuzzy heads peeked over its edge.

I walked toward the old shop. Red ants toiled over the ground near the corner of the storm cellar, toting tiny pebbles of rose and white quartz up their immense mound. Although much larger, this had to be the same hill whose residents my cousins and I had tormented that Thanksgiving all those years before. Clark sat on the hill when he was two, a story Mom had told just the previous Christmas, her eyes damp from both laughter and her loss, and from his pain, which she remembered as if it were her own.

Although I was home again last summer, I didn't go back out to the old place. I prefer remembering it when we lived there, as I have found myself doing more and more often this fall, as the air grows crisp and the somberness looms. This Thanksgiving I'll spend in the city, where, like the ground, my ties seem smoothed over, my present unruffled. There will be an afternoon of companionship with colleagues who, like me, have no history here. The kingbirds will spend the day in Texas, or wherever it is they migrate winters. Some fall, after all the fieldwork is done, the farmer who owns our old farmstead will throw one end of log chain around the locust tree, loop the other end over his tractor hitch, and pull the birds' home down. He'll soak some rags in diesel fuel and set fire to ours.

I prefer envisioning a natural, or supernatural, combustion—lightning or the light of stars magnified—but I am jumping ahead, I guess, to the final verdict, when the deer's home is gone, when the yellow wheat that engulfed it is forgotten, when only the ants survive, emerging from their underground tunnels to have their day.

⌄

Julene Bair's *essays and stories have appeared in many publications, including the* Missouri Review *and the* Chicago Tribune. *This essay comes from her book,* One Degree West: Reflections of a Plainsdaughter, *which won the 1998 Mid-List Press First Series Award in Creative Nonfiction. A graduate of both the Iowa Writers' Workshop and the Iowa Nonfiction Writing Program, she now lives in Laramie, Wyoming, with her son.*

September in South Dakota

Sheryl L. Nelms

there is ice
on the west wind

slivers stab through the evening air
threaten my garden

I whirry to gather the green
tomatoes in bushel baskets
wrap each in newspaper
to stow in burlap
in the basement

pick the zucchini
to grate and
bake
into bread
for the freezer

pull the last
of the beets
to pickle

mulch the strawberries

retreat to
the porch

to watch
the geese

going south

Originally from Kansas, **Sheryl L. Nelms** attended college in South Dakota and now lives in Texas. She has published more than four thousand poems, articles, and short stories, and makes her living as an insurance adjuster.

Fire Crazy

NANCY SATHER

In this story, Nancy Sather explores what it would be like to grow up in a family involved in prairie protection in a county where most people use their land for growing crops or raising livestock. Although the incidents in the story are fictitious, the natural resources, methods of prairie manage-ment, and opportunities for prairie protection are real.

⌄

"Some people's dads are crazy."

The minute the school bus door pulled shut, Jimmy Torblaa was hounding Jenny about her dad. He ran his fingers through his curly, corn-colored hair, and smirked. "My dad says someday your dad will get arrested. Someday they'll send him to jail for arson."

Jenny slipped into the window seat by her best friend, Margie, and pretended not to hear. But the words burned in her ears. Why couldn't Jimmy let her alone? It was embarrass-ing for a thirteen-year-old girl to have a match-happy dad, even when she knew he really wasn't crazy.

For as long as Jenny could remember, Dad had burned the pas-ture. The first time she was just six years old. Sitting in the school bus today, red faced with embarrassment, she clearly remembered her first conversation with her parents about prairie fire. That time the argument had been about Smokey the Bear.

"What about Smokey?" Jenny had asked.

"Smokey?"

"Smokey the Bear. He wouldn't like this. You're supposed to be careful with fire."

That's when Dad sat her down for a long history lesson. He explained how lightning has been setting prairies on fire for thousands of years. He told her how Indians burned the prairies to green up the grass and make it grow bigger to lure the bison. And he explained how fires can be planned and controlled.

Then her parents had started to argue. Dad thought May was the time to burn. Mom thought April.

"When I was a child in North Dakota, my folks always burned the coulee in April," said Mom. "It greened up the grass for the cattle."

"That was North Dakota," retorted Dad. "This is Minnesota. We need to burn late enough to set back the willows and aspen. Otherwise the whole place will go to brush."

They settled for the last week of April. Everybody had matches. And everybody had a water bucket, except Grandpa Jack, whom Dad called the "fire boss" because he had a broken ankle and couldn't run around. He stood by the pasture fence cheering them on.

"Prairie! Good wild prairie! There goes the reason I never improved that pasture," he bellowed with delight as the first, and only, thin line of fire cut through the prairie grass. It had fizzled out. Jenny never needed her water bucket. Dad said there wasn't enough grass to carry the fire. They'd need to hold back the cows at the end of the summer and let the grass grow taller before they tried it again.

Everything seemed backward. *Starting* fires! Keeping cattle *out* of a pasture! Grandpa seemed glad not to have improved the pasture. But Jenny thought improving something meant making it better. Why would Grandpa not want to make it better?

"What does *improving* a pasture mean?" asked Jenny.

"Planting exotic grass," said Dad.

Exotic grass? Jenny had visions of hula dancers in grass skirts.

"Grasses that don't belong in Minnesota prairies," said Mom. "Grasses that farmers plant in overused pastures to get a longer season. It's not really good for the prairie. If you graze the prairie just enough you can keep it as a pasture and still have native grasses. That's the trick."

One day when they were eight, Jenny and her friend Margie searched the pasture to see what was growing there. In the places where Dad held back the cattle, they found grass as tall as their heads, and wildflowers—orange lilies, yellow daisies with brown centers, spikes of pink flowers.

Jenny brought home a bouquet. Grandpa turned off the TV and went into his bedroom. He came back with a little black book, about four inches long and three inches high. The title was embossed in big gold letters. It said, *Flower Guide: Wildflowers East of the Rockies.*

"This belonged to your great-grandma," said Grandpa Jack. He pointed to the scrawly writing on the front page where it said, *"Anna Signe Nelson. From Papa, June 10, 1920, my birthday."*

Mom beamed at the bouquet. "Black-eyed Susans," she said, "and Philadelphia lily and blazing star. And the grasses are big bluestem and Indian grass."

"Those are the grasses that tickled the horses' bellies when *my* grandpa settled the plains," proclaimed Grandpa Jack with zest.

The spring that Jenny was ten, Dad woke her up before dawn to go hide in a tent in the pasture and watch the prairie chickens dance. She tried to explain it to Margie in a way that wouldn't sound funny. She told her how you had to sneak out in the dark. She described how the chickens blew up their cheeks like red balloons and pranced around.

That same year, Mom got homesick for North Dakota and scoured the prairie for pasqueflowers. Grandpa called them crocus.

"It's too wet," she said, returning empty-handed.

"You just go up in Torblaa's pasture on the beach ridge and you'll find plenty of those crocus," said Grandpa Jack. "They need that dry gravel soil. Lots of range plants used to grow up there—gaillardia, even skeleton weeds. You'll see lots of birds, too. I saw an upland plover on his fence post just the other day. Listen carefully and you can hear it call—*Quail-ee*."

"Better not go chasing for flowers or birds on Torblaa's land," warned Dad. "He's likely to run you off with his .22. He's got a notion the only thing that belongs in that pasture is him and some cows."

"Don't be too hard on the man," said Mom. "Those sandy ridges don't give him any cropland. We're lucky we have the potatoes and wheat for backup."

Grandpa agreed that Jenny should keep her exploring to their own pasture. If she'd just take her time she'd find plenty of treasure in their own forty acres. "It's a gold mine of nature! Just you wait! One of these days your dad's efforts will pay off and we'll find something really rare out there. All those prairie seeds have just been waiting in the soil for some fire to set them growing. That's one of the miracles of prairie fire, it gets those seeds going. Makes the grasses and flowers bear more seed, too. Now *that's* what I call improving a prairie! Restore it to the way it was, not run it to ruin with too many cows!"

Soon after, Jenny did find something precious. At least that was the way Grandpa and Mom acted about the tiny white lady slippers she found in the wet road ditch by the pasture. Grandpa thought they were so special he got in a fight with Harvey Bly over them.

"He's spraying the roadside! *Spraying*, I said!" Grandpa said one day after he'd driven out to the mailbox. Harvey was in charge of maintaining the county road.

Then Grandpa and Mom were out the door. Mom still had cookie dough on her fingers. Grandpa tore down the drive at fifty miles an hour, leaving a whirl of dust. He and Mom sat in the ditch by the lady slippers for an hour, refusing to move until Harvey and his spray truck were gone.

Sometimes Jenny thought that maybe her family *was* crazy.

As the years passed, Jenny started to enjoy the excitement of the fire season. It began to feel as regular as planting potatoes, or going to the county fair, or attending the fall bazaar at church or even the Christmas pageant.

The only difference was that burning in Jenny's household wasn't a once-a-season thing. It had grown from a little match in the April grass to a big yearlong production. In the fall, Grandpa mowed firebreaks all around the inside of the pasture fence. Biologists came from the city and sat around on winter evenings eating Mom's fried chicken, signing papers about protecting the prairie, and helping Dad make burn plans. Dad went off to "burn school" for a week and came back full of talk about fuel and backfires. By mid-April, Grandpa was glued to the weather forecasts. They needed a day that wouldn't rain but wasn't too hot or windy. The minute the weather looked right, Mom rushed to the fire warden for burn permits. Ladies from the town garden club turned up in their grubbiest clothes and headed for the pasture with shovels and backpack sprayers. Jenny and Mom were in charge of the back-fires. They set the little fire in a line on the east. Dad used his new drip torch to set the big fire on the west, so the wind could carry it across the pasture. Their little backfire would creep slowly like an orange slithering snake toward the big fire. When the fires met, there was no grass left. "No fuel," as Dad put it. The little backfire helped the big fire burn itself out.

As Jenny had grown older, the arguments about the pas-ture had changed. Now they weren't about burning; that was taken for granted. The argument was about what her parents called prairie management. Mom suggested that they should take the cows out of the pasture altogether.

Dad drew the line. "I need that grass," he said. "Don't know how I can ranch without it."

"Maybe you don't need to ranch any more," Mom said. "Your potatoes seem to be doing fine."

"So I'm supposed to plow it up?" Dad yelled. "Turn it into a potato field? Is that what you want?"

"No," Jenny heard herself say. No for the balloon-faced prairie chickens. No for the little lady slippers by the fence, the lilies, the blazing stars, the blue-purple gentians that bloomed late in fall. No for her secret flower—the tall, white, fragrant or-chid she found one July evening by the edge of a little wet swale. It was bigger and prettier than any orchid in her book. When she went online at school she found a picture of that plant: the western prairie fringed orchid. They had an endangered species in their pasture! Maybe this was what Grandpa Jack meant by treasure. No, Dad should not plow it up. She should be part of the discussion, because someday it would be hers. In the end, the prairie stayed but the cows went.

Jenny remembered all of this as she pretended not to hear Jimmy Torblaa on the bus. His taunts left her feeling mixed up. Didn't he know there were great things to see on the prairie? The girls in Jenny's class all thought Jimmy was cute. So why did he have to tease her in front of the other kids?

"Jimmy's just a creep," Margie whispered in Jenny's ear.

"Yeah," Jenny said, looking out the window as they passed by a big farm. But part of her knew why Jimmy was mad.

It had started at the end of the summer. One day, Jimmy's dad stopped by their house looking anxious. He asked if he could rent "that old no-good pasture" that her Dad wasn't using. It was a bad year for grass, and Mr. Torblaa's cattle were starving. If they couldn't get more grass he might have to sell them. Their farm would go under.

"It's not a pasture," said Dad. "It's a prairie. And it's not for rent. I have an agreement with the state to keep it in prairie and harvest it for prairie seed."

"You're crazy," blasted Mr. Torblaa. "Crazy no-good farmers. Under the influence of city folks. Can't even help out a neighbor. One of these days . . ."

Jenny knew Jimmy was scared Mr. Torblaa would have to sell his cows, but she didn't like being blamed. It wasn't her fault that Great-Grandma Anna had loved the flowers so much that they had never plowed the prairie. It wasn't her fault that Grandpa Jack had refused to improve the pasture. It wasn't her fault that Mom and Dad had become prairie managers. It wasn't her fault that prairies had been burning for ten thousand years and needed fire to flourish.

Then there was the problem with Jimmy and the sandhill cranes. One evening Dad had come in all aglow with excitement. "Grab your jacket, Jenny. You have to see these cranes! You don't see a bird this big walking around in the fields every day!"

Three long-legged, long-necked gray cranes were stalking around in the harvested wheat field. When they saw Dad and Jenny they flew into the middle of the prairie. Soon others joined them. Each time a new batch of the huge birds approached there was a raucous bugling call. A bird would break away from the group in the pasture and stalk out to greet the newcomers. Then they'd all walk back in a solemn procession.

"What are they doing, Dad?"

"They're staging for migration. Getting ready to fly. They'll be gone in a few days, over to the wildlife area and off to Texas. They're cousins of the whooping crane, you know."

But Jimmy Torblaa hadn't been happy about the "monster birds." He claimed they swooped into his father's pasture and ate up all the grass. His dad was really mad. He told Jenny that those monster birds had better not come out of her pasture again or her dad would hear about it! Jimmy even hinted that he might get rid of them himself, with his gun.

Jenny spent three days after school anxiously watching the birds. What if he was serious? She wanted the cranes to stay so she could watch them. But she was scared of what Jimmy might do and felt relieved the day they left.

The bus pulled up in front of Jimmy's house, and he made his way to the door. "Your dad's just a prairie pyromaniac," he said to Jenny as he passed.

"He gets a burning permit!" she finally yelled in her father's defense.

"Someday he won't," taunted Jimmy, "and the

fire department will have to come. And he'll have to pay."

It was strangely quiet when Jenny and Margie got off the bus at Jenny's stop. Dad and Mom were gone. Grandpa was napping. Even in early September the sky was hot. Tornado weather, Mom called this. She always said it was "the calm before the storm." Jenny could imagine that back in the days of the bison a prairie fire might pour across the plains on a day like this. Except that there wasn't any wind today. The grass was still too green to burn. A fire wouldn't carry very far.

As Jenny and Margie neared the house, they spied a thin trail of smoke in the corner of the prairie. In September? Dad never burned in September. You couldn't get a permit when it was this hot and dry. Besides, he planned to harvest the prairie seed. A man from the state highway department had already been around to buy it. He wouldn't burn before the harvest.

"Grandpa!" yelled Jenny. "The prairie's on fire! Quick, Margie, grab those shovels. I'll fill the backpack sprayers." The girls raced to the shed where Dad kept the burn equipment. Grandpa started up the pickup. "Matches," Jenny yelled. "We'll need to set a backfire."

Minutes later they watched the flames die away slowly in a notch between a slough and the backfire. "It's a good thing that man Torblaa doesn't know anything about burning prairies," said Grandpa. "Guess he doesn't know how green grass won't carry a fire, especially when it's headed for a pond."

By the time they got back to the house, smoky and dirty, Dad and Mom were home.

"It was set," said Grandpa grimly.

"And I know who did it," said Jenny.

"Then forget," said Dad. "You did a good job. The fire's out. Nobody's hurt and there's been no fire trucks or tractors driving around on the prairie, tearing up the sod and ruining my seed. We'll call this thing done."

A few minutes later, the fire department arrived.

"What are you doing here?" asked Grandpa.

Mr. Emory, the town fire chief, looked grim. "There's a fire in your pasture."

"Do you see smoke?" asked Dad. "Do you see flames?"

The firefighters looked skeptical. "But Ted Torblaa called!"

"Oh," said Dad, "sorry he wasted your time. Mistakes happen."

A week later, Dad was combining prairie seed. Mr. Torblaa drove by and leaned out the window of his truck. Jimmy watched Jenny from his perch on a pile of feed sacks in the back.

"You've got to be out of your gourd!" said Mr. Torblaa.

"Thirteen dollars a pound for this seed," said Dad. "And no taxes on prairie land. If you'd stick to burning your own pasture, and do it in the spring, you might be able to bring the prairie back there, too. This is a rich batch of seed. Thirteen species of grass, and—Jenny counted them—thirty-two species of wildflowers."

At first Mr. Torblaa didn't seem to be listening. But Jenny's dad kept talking.

"Dry prairie like yours has a whole batch of plants good for roadsides. Not too tall. There are programs that pay a man to keep the land in prairie. You could call tomorrow."

Mr. Torblaa looked thoughtful. Finally he said, "I'll have to talk to the missus."

Talk to the missus! Jenny knew he was hedging. That's how farmers hedged when they wanted to say yes, but not right now. Mrs. Torblaa's main concern was her job in town. She wouldn't care about the pasture. Maybe that meant Mr. Torblaa was actually considering her dad's advice!

"Jimmy here could go to burn school with me someday," Jenny's dad said.

Jimmy gave a slight smile. For the first time, Jenny noticed the dimples in his cheeks and the blueness of his eyes. Blue as gentians on the prairie! She couldn't help smiling back.

"You know, there are badgers in our pasture," Jimmy said to her then. "They waddle funny. If you wanted, you could come over and see them."

"Thanks," Jenny said with a smile. "I'd like that."

❧

Nancy Sather *is a native of the prairie region of northwest Minnesota, where she has worked as a plant ecologist for the past decade. Her poems, essays, and articles have been published in a variety of literary magazines and in the* Minnesota Conservation Volunteer. *She lives in Minneapolis with her sons and an ever changing menagerie of pets.*

How to Replant a Prairie

Neal Smith National Wildlife Refuge, Prairie City, Iowa

ANN LYNN

First, harvest the beans.
Haul away refrigerators,
old cars, wringer washers
from the fields
and gulches.

Then you must find
the native seeds.
Comb cemeteries,
railroad beds.
With practice
you'll learn to recognize
the moment when the seeds
will fall.

To the planting, invite fiddlers
and a throng of people.
Give each a bag
filled with seeds:
partridge pea,
blazing star,
pearly everlasting.

Tell them to throw
seeds into the air,
dance them into the ground.

Ann Lynn *has worked as a social worker, editor, and freelance
writer, and now teaches poetry writing to children. Her poems are
published or forthcoming in literary journals, including* River Oak
Review, Defined Providence, Hawai'i Review, *and* Many Mountains Moving. *Much of her work is about her family.*

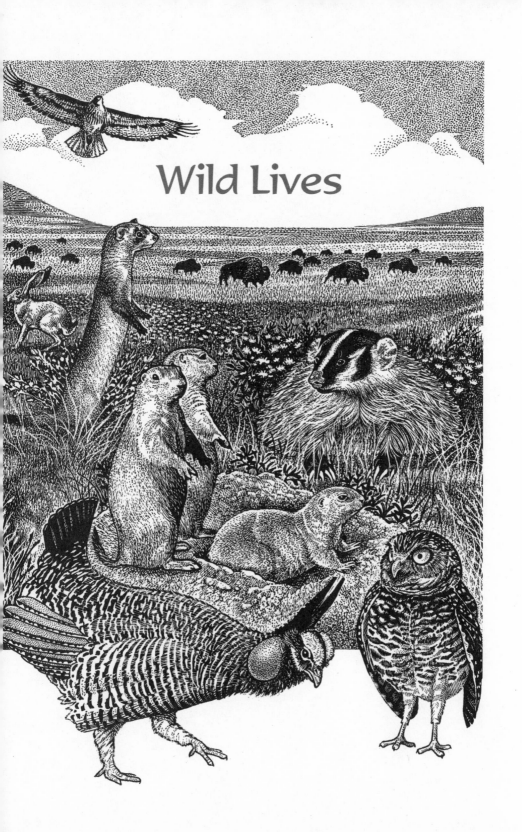

Wild Lives

Snow Print Two: Hieroglyphics

BARBARA JUSTER ESBENSEN

In the alley
under the last cold rung
of the fire escape
birds are printing
the new snow
with a narrow alphabet.

Their scribbled secrets
tell of lost songs
and the howling wind
that claws like a cat.

These are messages
from the small dark birds
to me.

Barbara Juster Esbensen *was a teacher, a poet-in-residence, and the author of more than a dozen books of fiction and poetry for children. She lived in Minneapolis.*

Nature's Ways

SANORA BABB

Sanora Babb was seven in 1914 when her family moved from a small town in Oklahoma to an isolated homestead on the Colorado plains. Her memoir, An Owl on Every Post, *describes her family's experiences living in a one-room dugout on the arid and windswept prairie. In this excerpt from her memoir, Sanora responds to the death of her favorite horse, Fred.*

The next morning at dawn, before going to the creek for water, the men hitched Dip and Bugs to the doubletrees and walked them out to where Fred lay dead. Bugs snorted and flattened his ears. Dip whinnied and reared and tried to break free. After quieting the fearful horses, the men secured Fred's great stiff body with ropes and chains and dragged him a mile away into a draw.

"It's a wonder the coyotes didn't try to eat him in the night," Mama said.

I ran to the barn and cried, and cried more when I saw the long white hairs from his mane, hardly noticed before, caught in the rough boards of the stall. Bounce came in and nudged me, then stood back, his tail down, wagging slowly to express his sympathy.

We left the barn and walked into the field. Our broomcorn was higher than my head. The rising sunlight filtered down through the green blades, the field was fragrant with morning. A grasshopper flew onto my dress. He looked at me, his eyes direct and impertinent, as if he knew everything I did not. Then he spat his "tobacco juice": his comment on my grief in the natural world of so much birthing, hatching, eating, dying.

When the men returned and hitched the horses to the wagon for their trip to the creek for water, I waited until they drove out the gate before Bounce and I ran after them. The spicy fragrance of sage was in the air. Soapweeds, as we called yucca, had lost their creamy blooms. In the spring Grandfather had showed me the moth that pollinates the yuccas and taught me the parts of the flowers.

"No accident, either," he said. "That moth has a special kind of mouth for gathering yucca pollen off the stamen. She carries it to another yucca flower and takes great care to place it just where it belongs on the stigma. In 1872 a Professor Riley found that out. I read about it and never forgot it because it just goes to show there's a pattern. Pull a few threads and you undo nature's pattern. Understand?"

"What if she goes to another kind of flower?" I asked.

"She doesn't. She and the yucca can't live without each other. You see, when she lays her eggs in the seed capsules, she has already provided her children with food by pollination for the new seeds. And there's plenty of seed for her young and for new yuccas, too."

I wanted very much to know how the insect knew to do this, but all Grandfather could say was, "That's Nature." The number of Nature's secrets multiplied; sometimes it seemed to me that we were more ignorant than the creatures and plants.

The prairie dog town we passed on our way to the creek provided such entertainment that momentarily I forgot my sorrow. In summer these gay little marmots spent the hot afternoons in their burrows, coming out to search for food in the mornings and late afternoons. They ate seeds and grass, the good buffalo grass that was highly nutritious the year

round, even when it was brown and dry. The water in these was all they needed. Fat and furry, their cheek pouches full, hundreds were feeding, each close to his mound of earth tunneled from the ground. Posted sentinels sat up on their hind legs, their bright, intelligent eyes watching our approach to determine if we were among their enemies—coyotes, badgers, eagles, and hawks. In the fall, rattlesnakes sometimes moved into abandoned holes, often forcing the abandonment. Among the prairie dogs a jackrabbit was feeding, his fur blending with the dun summer grass, only his long ears moving. Suddenly Bounce sprang into the town after the "jack," who leaped into the air and ran in great bounds, quickly outdistancing the dog. He stopped abruptly, sat up and looked back, then ran on. At this commotion, the prairie dog sentinels gave their shrill warning call. The quick little animals sped to their burrows, sat up for an instant to sound the alarm, and with a flick of their short tails, they dove into the earth. They must have turned about at once for heads appeared for a cautious glance, then they sprang back onto their mounds, looked all about and returned to their feeding, or comic antics, leaving the watch to their sentries. Through all this they appeared quick and bold and cheerful. When really frightened, as by a rattlesnake taking over his burrow, the little prairie dog stood his ground and chattered in outraged protest, before he bowed to the inevitable. Then he accepted his dispossession and dug himself another home, deep, with many side chambers, forming the unearthed dirt into a flood-proof mound.

The rangy jackrabbit that had escaped stopped under a sagebrush and continued his feeding. Unlike the cottontail, it was not his habit to seek safety in a hole.

At the creek the horses were freed to drink and rest under

the cottonwoods while Grandfather and Papa filled the barrels with cold, clean water. Bounce and I waded in the shallow stream, he playfully trying to catch minnows.

I came out of the water to talk to Bugs, who did not respond.

"We'll kill him with kindness," Papa called.

I thought of Fred, so responsive, and it seemed to me that Dip was thinking of him too, for he stood with lowered head, now and then giving a great sigh. I pressed my face against his warm neck to hide my renewing tears.

"None of that," Grandfather scolded. "We'll rest a spell," he said to Papa, and came over to me, thumping my shoulder with his knuckles. "You are ordinarily a cheerful girl. Now, you will just have to get used to Nature's ways."

"I hate Nature's ways!"

"Well, you are one of them. And let me tell you, little miss, 'hate' is bad medicine. You'll do well to think that over."

"But I love Fred!"

"If you will stop these infernal tears"—Grandfather lowered his voice, which was already low—"I may go on a little jaunt tonight, and you may go with me."

❧

So at last I was permitted to go for a night walk with Grandfather. When he opened the door, the light from our room in the earth leaped into the dark, and we with it; when he closed the door, the light was pressed back as into a box. We stood in the night. I saw nothing in that blackness, but I heard the horses in the barn nosing the hay, blowing against their lips with a peaceful rippling sound.

Grandfather did not go through the west gate but struck off across the cane patch to the south. The cane was tall and cool. Walking along the rows, brushing against the crisp leaves, smelling the cane's green fragrance, I knew my way. Field mice squeaked and ran, their feet making small soft sounds. Bounce followed stealthily although he had been forbidden this particular jaunt. At the fence, Grandfather stepped on the lowest barbed wire and held the middle one up for me to go through, then he half-stepped, half-leaped over the top wire.

Our eyes had grown used to the dark; the dark had a sheen from the stars. Ahead, Grandfather walked as if to a destination, the sound of his long steps guiding me. Bounce stayed close at my heels and I was glad. I was not afraid of the night; I liked being in it, but this was no ordinary walk. I had wondered all summer about these night walks and now felt a sense of promise and portent. The moon slid up fast from another region, revealing the straight horizon a world away. Black shadows appeared beside the scattered sage and soapweeds, but the big plain lay under the moonlight in opal clarity.

Walking was easier now. I could see the grass-blades and the tough little weeds resting from the day's wind. Grandfather had told me they were not resting but growing: "Plants do their growing at night." I stopped to watch a milkweed grow, but nothing was disclosed to me beyond an exchange of affection. The scent of skunk drifted by, refined by distance. Bounce lifted his dog nose into the air current but did not leave me. Because of our loitering, Grandfather was far ahead, and we ran to catch up, avoiding the prickly-pear cactus that grew in clumps of runners close to the ground, its thick oval leaves dangerous with thorns that pierced and ached the flesh, as I knew from experience.

Grandfather's lean frame cast a long black shadow. I watched my own and the dog's shadow gliding along. Bounce and I sensed our privilege to this journey depended upon our making no sounds other than our breath and the soft pad of our feet. We were following someone we loved, but we were drawn nearer to each other in the wake of that tall man's solitude.

We had been walking toward the part of the creek where we bathed and from which we hauled water. There the banks sloped gently down to the stream where horses and wagons forded the shallow water. Willows and cottonwoods lined the shore, and wild onions and red sand poppies grew there. Killdeers ran crying bleakly, and bats flew at dusk. But Grandfather veered off to the southeast where there were no trails, past a prairie dog town of many mounds. The little bushy-tailed rodents were asleep in their burrows, but here and there a small billy owl sat on the mound of an abandoned hole he had taken for his home. Once we surprised a large badger on his night hunt, and Grandfather turned with a sharp command to Bounce. In a fight the badger could have torn Bounce apart with his sharp claws, but he chose to dig rapidly into the earth, ignoring us. Farther along we saw three coyotes relaying in pursuit of a jackrabbit. After that the plain seemed deserted except for occasional small rustlings and the running of small feet.

There was nothing in sight on the open prairie. The high clear air shimmered with moonlight. The silence deepened into a sound of itself, a palpable atmosphere through which we walked to what destination I did not know. In this unpeopled place what destination could there be? An intensely felt but not understood part of me was being stretched in every direction to the circular horizon and upward to that immense field of stars. I was aware of my hunger then, a hunger that stirred me to living life, a knowledge that I was more than myself, that self of the hours of day and night, that the unknown answer lay all about me, that everything spoke to me and yet I could not understand. I wanted to be alone with this new feeling, but I was overcome with such a loneliness that I dared to run ahead and slip my hand into Grandfather's. His dry fingers bent to enclose my hand that sought his finite touch and comfort. We walked like this until we neared the length of prairie that broke off at a precipice, a long high cliff following the creekbed far below. He let go my hand and walked more slowly, scuffing over the grass here and there, feeling for button cactus. He sat down, raised his knees, and let his arms rest upon them. A sigh came out of his slackened body. He motioned for me to sit near him and for Bounce to lie down at his feet. We sat looking into the nothingness of night. We listened to baby coyotes yipping over a kill their parents had brought them.

As an adult, **Sanora Babb** *worked for small-town newspapers, as a country schoolteacher, and as a college writing teacher. During the Great Depression, she worked in the California fields setting up government camps for migrant workers. She also traveled extensively with her cinematographer husband, James Wong Howe. In addition to* An Owl on Every Post, *she has written a novel, two collections of short stories, and a poetry collection. She lives in Hollywood.*

Migration Prayer:
The Geese Speak

CYNTHIA PEDERSON

weighed by this scale of sky

    too heavy   too heavy

        we spill

cup us
in your glacial palm
let us sink
into the ice-carved heart
of these hills
welcome us with water

let the darkness
of a wing-worn sky
brood above us

and in this patient prairie
may we rest

Cynthia Pederson *was raised in Topeka, Kansas. From her familiar Flint Hills, she left to live in Belcourt, North Dakota, on an Ojibwa Indian Reservation, where she discovered and explored a different kind of prairie. This poem was written while she lived in the Turtle Mountains of north-central North Dakota.*

The Lesson of the Birds

A Pawnee Story

Because trees are scarce on the prairie, many of the region's birds make their nests on the ground. But that means the parent birds have to be especially vigilant about protecting their eggs and young.

One day a man whose mind was open to the teaching of the powers wandered on the prairie. As he walked, his eyes upon the ground, he spied a bird's nest hidden in the grass, and arrested his feet just in time to prevent stepping on it. He paused to look at the little nest tucked away so snug and warm, and noted that it held six eggs and that a peeping sound came from some of them. While he watched, one moved, and soon a tiny bill pushed through the shell, uttering a shrill cry. At once the parent birds answered, and he looked up to see where they were. They were not far off; they were flying about in search of food, chirping the while to each other and now and then calling to the little one in the nest.

The homely scene stirred the heart and the thoughts of the man as he stood there under the clear sky, glancing upward toward the old birds and then down to the helpless young in the nest at his feet. As he looked, he thought of his people, who were so often careless and thoughtless of their children's needs, and his mind brooded over the matter. After many days he desired to see the nest again, so he went to the place where he had found it, and there it was as safe as when he left it. But a change had taken place. It was now full to overflowing with little birds, who were stretching their wings, balancing on their little legs and making ready to fly, while the parents with encouraging calls were coaxing the fledglings to venture forth.

"Ah!" said the man, "if my people would only learn of the birds, and, like them, care for their young and provide for their future, homes would be full and happy, and our tribe strong and prosperous."

When this man became a priest, he told the story of the bird's nest and sang its song; and so it has come down to us from the days of our fathers.

The Pawnees once lived near the Platte River in what is now Nebraska.

Wawaskesy, the Windrunner

GILLIAN RICHARDSON

Pronghorn, sometimes called antelope, are extremely fast runners. They can sustain speeds of thirty miles per hour and achieve bursts that are more than twice that fast. This story offers a glimpse into the life of a pronghorn on the Saskatchewan prairie.

Against the blaze of a prairie sunset trotted a low silhouette. The coyote stopped frequently, tilting her muzzle skyward. If telltale scents of a possible meal drifted in the cool spring air, she would intercept them sooner or later.

But even her keen nose could not detect the newcomer to this prairie night. Huddled among the sagebrush merely yards away, the pronghorn fawn gave off no odor. Wawaskesy lay motionless, a gray-brown lump like so many other mounds of earth. His instincts held him fast to the spot where his mother had left him, alone but cleverly protected by his camouflage. The coyote continued her trek along the horizon.

Through the night the ever-present wind skipped across the open plain, gently tossing the grasses around the sleeping day-old fawn. When the eastern sky softened to pink and mauve, Wawaskesy awoke, his large dark eyes and pointed ears alert to his mother's approach. She had spent the night grazing nearby. Now, before full daylight revealed her single fawn to the world, she returned to allow him to nurse.

The young pronghorn drank his fill, standing on angular legs that would soon carry him faster than a human could run. He gained strength by the hour. After one more night curled alone in the open, he would be ready to take up the nomadic life of the prairie pronghorn.

Wawaskesy spent his first weeks eating and resting. Soon he and his mother joined a small group of does with their young. While the adults grazed and kept watch, Wawaskesy jumped and ran with the other fawns. The youngsters' play taught them vital skills. Wawaskesy was the best at "chicken tag," leaping aside seconds before certain collision with another fawn. Someday the game might be a lifesaving trick. Nothing slowed the fawns; even resting does became boulders for jumping on and off.

Roaming the dry, shortgrass prairie with the herd, Wawaskesy ate sagebrush and wild onion, pea vine and alfalfa. Even cactus became a meal, its juice sometimes the only drink at hand. Wawaskesy grew quickly. His tan coat of stiff, hollow hairs protected him from the burning sun and drying winds. Later his coat would keep him warm when arctic blasts of winter brought numbing cold. He wore alternate bands of tan and white on his chest, and a black band covered his face from eyes to nose. When he matured next summer, Wawaskesy would sport a pair of branched horns that he'd shed each year.

On a mid-August day, a fretful wind began to rise. Far to the west, clouds covered the sun's face. Long before thunder rumbled, jagged spikes of lightning stabbed at the earth, and white light skittered along the underside of a massive cloud bank that crept relentlessly eastward.

The herd began to bunch together, moving south toward low hills that would give them some shelter from the coming storm. But something else was on the move, too, slicing across the rolling plain on rails of steel.

The eastbound freight train sped along, keeping just ahead of the storm. Wawaskesy had already seen trains at a distance; he had felt the ground shake and heard the deep-throated rumble of the engines. Instinct now warned the herd to hurry; the tracks lay across their path southward. As they ran, each adult flared the patch of white hairs on its rump, relaying the built-in warning signal throughout the herd. Nimble legs lifted the pronghorn easily over the ground until they fairly flew down dips and up rises. As the speed of the lead doe picked up, the others became strung out in snakelike fashion. Most of the young were near the front; Wawaskesy joined the end, near the buck pronghorn that always ran last when the herd was in flight.

The rain caught them on the final down slope to the tracks. Like knives before the wind, it slashed into the animals. Wawaskesy lost sight of the others in the confusion of driving rain, crashing thunder, and galloping freight train.

The sky boomed and sizzled, and the ground vibrated. The main pronghorn herd darted across the tracks moments ahead of the train. But Wawaskesy veered away, his only thought to escape the iron monster, the source of all his terror. He raced alongside the beast, trying to outrun the awful noise, the trembling under his hoofs.

The train stretched for more than a mile, and Wawaskesy began to tire. His pace slackened but not his fear. The storm closed in on the heels of the train. The howling wind whipped sheets of water across the land. Hard chunks of ice pelted Wawaskesy. The land turned white, the air freezing. The helpless pronghorn ran on, fueled by panic, heading away from the tracks at last. But by now he was several miles from his family and moving in the opposite direction.

Wawaskesy ran until his gasping lungs forced him to stop. Shivers of cold and fear gripped him. The hailstorm had been brief, but it had left him badly bruised. Now he stood alone, head down, every muscle screaming. His enemy vanished into the distance, ragged storm clouds following like dust behind a stampede.

Little warmth was left in the sun that day to heal Wawaskesy's hurts. Night found the lone pronghorn curled beside a slough, small shudders giving the only sign of life in his body. The tepid water of the shallow pond had been all that he could swallow. He was too exhausted to eat. The night was still after the fury of the day's events.

At sunup Wawaskesy stood, stretched painfully, and began to pick his way along a fence. It guided him eastward, and he wandered beside it, nibbling the tasty grasses that grew nearby. His strength slowly returned, and he began to take notice of his surroundings.

From the top of a rise, he saw animals scattered across a pasture. They looked somehow familiar, and the scent that reached him gave no reason for fear. He missed the company of the herd. He crawled under the bottom strand of fence wire and soon walked among the cattle. They took little notice of the stranger, and for the rest of the day, the animals grazed companionably. Wawaskesy found a sense of security in their midst.

The young pronghorn stayed among them for several weeks. He had no reason to move on. There was ample food that the cattle did not touch. He slept close to them, listening to the comforting sounds of their movements and grazing.

On a day when a soft, steady rain soaked the land, Wawaskesy became aware of sounds and smells that jarred his nerves. He had moved with the cattle until they approached the eastern edge of their fenced pasture. Beyond lay the buildings of an industrial complex on the outskirts of a small prairie city. The moisture in the air carried strange choking smells and harsh noises. It was as though a wall had risen before Wawaskesy to turn him back. He would go no closer.

Next morning, in the chill that made the grasses crisp beneath his hoofs, Wawaskesy's ears caught a sound that set his heart pounding. The roar rose in pitch, climbing into the air until it surrounded the pronghorn. Far too recent in Wawaskesy's memory was the horror of the train. He didn't wait to see this new monster. He began to run. Overhead, the jet gained altitude, then circled away to the north.

Once he was on the move, Wawaskesy felt suddenly free and sure of himself. His muscles were rested and strong. His instincts drove him, and he ran easily. Even after the dreaded rumbling had faded into nothing, he kept on. Wawaskesy had found his stride. He leaped a fence, then another, ran alongside the asphalt ribbon of highway, and at last clattered across it to head toward low hills in the southwest.

He spent that day alone and felt the nip of a frosty night. He saw each blade of grass sparkle as the first shafts of morning sun flooded across the land. His breath hung in small clouds before him.

Always now he moved west, drawn by a strange restlessness, guided by an instinct from the ancient past. He traveled steadily, pausing briefly here and there to nibble at the grass. The lush green of the land gave way to gold and brown, and large flocks of geese hurried by on the wind. Finally Wawaskesy saw where his journey would end.

Before him, spread across their winter range, were hundreds

of pronghorn. Wawaskesy knew his rightful place was with them. Ruled by ageless instincts, he had found his way home.

A former teacher-librarian, **Gillian Richardson** *now writes fiction and nonfiction for children. Three of her books have won the Canadian Children's Book Center's Our Choice Award. She lives in British Columbia.*

Prairie Dogs Live in Lubbock

WALT McDONALD

except a few hundred in colonies
near towns like Muleshoe, Midland,
and Littlefield. All others
have disappeared, starved by farmers,

poisoned, wiped out in thousands
by the plague that rides from colony
to colony like royalty
in the cushioned stomachs of fleas.

Ranchers hate varmints, losing good mounts,
forelegs snapped by their holes. Once,
boys could stand a mile out of town
and shoot at dogs with .22s all day.

Now, the city's Prairie Dog Town
has a wall and a law against molesting
the hundred rodents, which scamper
like rabbits, stand on hind legs,

and try to bark, and the dozen or so
owls that squat like ceramics.

Young couples bring their children
to feed prairie dogs once or twice

over the years. And sometimes
in the cool of evening, old people
driving slow will idle by the fence
and watch them bark awhile.

Walt McDonald *is the author of eighteen collections of poems and a professor of English and poet-in-residence at Texas Tech University in Lubbock.*

River Dance

ANN COOPER

Birds that migrate over the central United States stop to rest on rivers and pothole lakes throughout the prairie region. Because many rivers have been dammed and many lakes have been drained for agriculture, those that remain have become critical habitat for these feathered travelers.

The High Plains of Eastern Colorado are still locked in winter. It is mid-March, spring break, but it doesn't feel like spring. Swirls of snow from last week's storm fringe fence lines and gulches. Weeds and grasses along the highway are tawny yellow and dead. Away to the north, all we can see of the South Platte River is a snaking line of leafless cottonwoods. Outside, the temperature is about fifteen degrees and the wind is blowing. Brrr! Some people we know are heading west to the mountains to ski over spring break. Others are heading to warm places. We are zooming east on the interstate on our way to Kearney, Nebraska, to watch a very special dance.

The dancers are birds, sandhill cranes, thousands and thousands of them. In early spring they begin to migrate north to their nesting grounds. By the time they've flown nonstop about six hundred miles from west Texas or New Mexico, they're ready for a rest. Every year they stop along the Platte River valley. They choose places from Overton, west of Kearney, all the way to Grand Island. Here they spend a few weeks regaining energy and mingling with other cranes. At night they roost on sandbars in the river for safety. By day they eat. They need to refuel for the rest of their long journey. Sometimes they dance.

We arrive in the Kearney area in late afternoon. We leave the interstate to grab a quick snack at the gas station. Then we drive the back roads. Soon, among the cornstalks in a wintry-looking field, we see about fifty cranes. They are *very* large, gangly birds! Our field guide says greater sandhill cranes can be fifty inches tall. Wow! That's the height of an average second-grader. The cranes step through the stubble on long, spindly legs. Their feathers are grayish, some tinged with russet, and their tufty tails droop. They remind me of ostriches. Above their long beaks are bright red crown patches. The patches seem to glow in the late-afternoon slanted light. Through our binoculars, we can see that the patches are not feathery: they are bare skin!

We watch from the car. We don't want to disturb the cranes. This is their place. They act fidgety and they're quite noisy. Some are eating, gleaning leftover grain. Others are hustling and crowding each other. One leaps into the air, flapping its wings, its spindly legs dangling. Then it lands again. Now two are leaping and flapping together. The excitement seems to be catching. Soon, more cranes are leaping and landing, flapping and squawking. It's quite a dance! Actually, it's only practice. The males and females are pairing up. They are jittery with spring fever. The really serious mating dances get going later, on the nesting grounds in the north. But this dance we are watching is wild and crazy enough.

As dusk falls, the cranes leave the field to join other flocks overhead. They mill around. It looks as if they are trying to decide something. After a while they all fly off toward the river. And then it's dark.

Next morning, way before dawn, we bundle up to go and see the cranes at their nighttime roost. The chill cuts through all our layers of clothing. I have to scrunch my fingers inside my mittens and stick my hands deep in my pockets. My breath feels prickly and freezes in my nose. We hike to the river and out across it along an old railroad bridge. We can't use a light  and we can't talk. We mustn't disturb the roosting birds. They roost on the smooth sandbars out in the river, but we can't see anything yet. It's pitch black. Every so often a spooky warbling sound echoes from the river. Before we can see the slightest hint of light in the eastern sky, the cranes begin to stir. We stir, too. We jump up and down on the spot, trying to warm our toes without making a noise. It is so cold that our breath huffs out like dragon breath. In the half-light we can see that the cranes are fussing now, fluffing up their feathers, preening, and drinking, their long beaks ladling up water, pointing skyward as the drink trickles down their skinny throats.

The noise and restlessness increase. Groups of cranes leap up from the sandbars and circle. Their weird gargling *gar-rooooooo* sounds are unearthly and spine-chilling. We shiver with nice fright as well as cold. More cranes join the ones flying until the sky seems full of huge wings and straggly, "undercarriage" legs. Then, as if they shared one brain, they flap away toward the flooded meadows.

A crane expert tells us there is a famous saying about the Platte River, that it is "a mile wide and an inch deep, too thick to drink and too thin to plow." It does look brownish and thick—muddy. And it is quite wide where we walk. That's why the cranes like it here. The sandy islands are good roosts, safe from predators—especially since some of the cranes seem to act as "guard birds" all night. The expert says that long ago the river was wider than it is now. It used to flood often, washing away tree seedlings whose roots were trying to get a hold on the sandbars in the river channels. Now, people divert water from the river for farming. There are dams upstream. Without floods to wash away seedlings, tall willows and cottonwoods cover some islands. These places are no longer good crane habitat. The expert tells us cranes need shallow channels, bare sandbars and islands, and flooded meadows, where they can pick and peck to find worms and grubs. Most of all, the cranes need there to be enough water flowing to keep the Platte River a mile wide. A single, deep channel without sandbars is of no use to them.

It's light now, and all the cranes have left the sandbar roost. We drive the back roads some more, wanting to see the cranes dance again. By noon, it is even colder. An icy fog closes in and the snow begins to fall. We head home toward Denver, not wanting to be caught in a blizzard. Driving into the swirl of snow, we think about the cranes. We wonder how they'll do on their long, tough journey north through the still-wintry land ahead. We're glad they take their spring break in the Platte River valley, in areas set aside for them. Most of all, we're glad we got to see their most amazing river dance.

Ann Cooper, *past "Brit" and present ardent Coloradoan, is a teacher-on-the-trail and has written ten nature books for children. Her poetry and stories for children have appeared in several magazines, including* Spider, Ladybug, R-A-D-A-R, Friend, *and* Clubhouse.

Tumbleweeds

BEVERLY A. J. HALEY

Biologists in white jackets label it
Amaranthus albus;
but prairie people, who live with it,
know it as tumbleweed.

Summer-green, feathery bush plants break
whole from their roots in autumn winds.
Wild with sudden freedom, each plant, a skeleton
of its former self, dances with frenzy
across vast decaying fields and prairie,
whips along highways, snatching
the underpinnings of cars or trucks
for miles of joyriding, perhaps
cavorts with dozens of playmates
to entangle bikes and racks
or transform barbed-wire fences into fortress walls.

Some snuggle together in hidden hollows
to hibernate for the winter.

Having lived all her life on the prairie, **Beverly A. J. Haley** *writes of the place and the people whose lives are defined by its harsh yet beautiful simplicity. Her work has appeared in such sources as* Cattle Country News, New Mexico Magazine, Empire, *and* South Dakota Magazine.

In the Open

KATHLEEN NORRIS

In her book Dakota, *Kathleen Norris reflects on how the life and land-scape of the Great Plains influences the human spirit. The following is one chapter from that book.*

⌣

There are an estimated 5,000 antelope in Perkins County, South Dakota, and about 3,900 people. Antelope are like grace notes on the land: small and quick and bold. When threatened they take the high ground. They confounded Meriwether Lewis when he and William Clark first encountered them near the White River in September of 1804:

> We found the Antelope extreemly shye and
> watchfull . . . I got within about 200 paces of them
> when they smelt me and fled; I gained the top of the
> eminence on which they stood, as soon as possible
> from whence I had an extensive view of the country the
> antilopes which had disappeared in a steep reveene
> now appeared at a distance of about three miles on the
> side of a ridge—so soon had these antelopes gained the
> distance I doubted at ferst that they were the same I
> had just surprised, but my doubts soon vanished when

I beheld the rapidity of their flight . . . it appeared
reather the rappid flight of birds.

Seeing antelope bound across a field quickens my heart; I
long to go with them. It's like the feeling I used to have when
I was a kid playing outdoors, that I never wanted to go in, that
I could stay outside and somehow become part of that world;
grass, wind and trees, day and night itself.

I get that feeling now when I'm in the open, walking in the
country around my prairie town. The land, the 360 degrees of
unobstructed horizon, invites you to keep on walking. The
light is continually changing: shadows of cloud move fast on
the land, coloring it slate blue. A sudden break in the cloud
cover turns a butte chalk white; a cloudburst in the distance
unleashes sheets of rain, and you study it carefully for the telltale white sheen that means hail. A person could stand and
watch this changing land and sky forever.

Even on very cold days (and my gauge for that is an infor-
mal one: if my eyebrows start to ache, it's below zero), coming
back into a house feels all wrong. It is hard to turn back to the
human world of ceiling and walls and forced air heating.

I know the shock of hitting paved road after riding grass-
track roads and walking in the country all day. The rhythm of
the tires on the two-lane blacktop says to me: *civilization, town,
other people,* and I don't want that. As when I was a child, I want
to remain in the open, becoming something other than human under the sky.

Maybe it's our sky that makes us crazy. We can see the
weather coming, and we like it that way. Being truly of the
Plains, however, means something more. It's the old North

Dakota farmer asked by a sociologist why he hasn't planted trees around his farmhouse. No shelterbelt, not even a shade tree with a swing for his children. "Don't like trees," he said, "they hem you in."

Kathleen Norris *lives in Lemmon, South Dakota. She is the author of two books of poetry and several books of nonfiction, including* Dakota: A Spiritual Geography.

Coyote Hunts

NANCY DAWSON

Coyotes are resourceful and adaptable predators that live in a variety of habitats, including the prairie. Nancy Dawson wrote this story after seeing a lean coyote snap at the tail feathers of a magpie one winter day.

Coyote wakes to the whines of her five pups. Her mate has not yet returned to the den with food, and the pups are hungry.

She leaves to hunt alone. Soon, the pups will go with their parents and learn to hunt, but today, they are still too young to leave the protection of the den.

Coyote roams the prairie, searching for food under the afternoon sun. She must feed herself first so that she will have the strength to hunt for her pups. Far to the south, her mate is also on the prowl.

Coyote leaps up and snatches a grasshopper in mid-flight. A crunchy snack, but that is all. She trots on, padded paws avoiding patches of prickly pear cactus.

She watches eagle's flight to see where and what he is hunting. But eagle disappears behind the chalky buttes that rise straight up from the flat prairie. Coyote overturns a rock and slurps up the scurrying bugs before trotting on in search of more substantial food.

She sees the silhouette of a female pronghorn antelope standing on a distant hill. Pronghorn is too big and too fast for coyote to catch, but if its young are lying on the prairie nearby, maybe coyote can snatch one.

She circles to the south, sneaking closer. She sniffs the air, but smells only grasses and flowers. She scans the prairie for baby pronghorn shapes, but there are many patches of brown earth among the green short grasses, and none of the patches move.

Pronghorn spies coyote's approach from her hilltop lookout. She leaps in the air and rushes coyote. Coyote veers north, chased by pronghorn. Coyote runs west, turns, and charges after pronghorn. They zigzag east and south, west and north, pursuing each other over the wide prairie. Pronghorn speeds off into the distance.

Exhausted and panting, coyote slinks south, her bushy tail dragging. After coyote is gone, pronghorn returns to nuzzle her twins where they crouch motionless on the open prairie.

Coyote pauses next to some rocks in the late afternoon shade. But she cannot rest long. She must find food for herself and her hungry pups.

She moves on, following the scent of deer mouse to its nest. Coyote pounces and gulps down four babies.

Krrr! Krrr! Kree! A female mountain plover calls to her mate. The plump brown bird is nestled on the bare ground, incubating her eggs. Coyote races toward the nest just as plover flies high into the sky.

Krrr! Krrr! Kree! Plover screeches as she dives back down to earth some distance away. She lands with a Plop! and drags what looks like a broken wing as she crawls along the prairie. Coyote runs forward at top speed and leaps, but catches only air and dirt. Plover flies far away, leaving her fake injury and a hungry coyote behind.

Coyote turns back, scanning the brown prairie for signs of the plover's nest. But plover has lured her too far away.

Coyote turns toward the narrow asphalt road, drawn by the scent of fresh roadkill. Raven and magpie are already there, fighting over the remains of a squashed rattlesnake. Coyote crouches in the ditch next to the road and slinks closer. She leaps forward and snaps her jaws, just missing magpie's long black tail feathers.

Coyote swallows the remains of snake and trots west. She sees her mate in the distance and travels south to join him.

Together, they slink toward a cluster of prairie dog mounds from downwind, to keep their coyote scent from announcing their presence. They crouch behind spiky yucca plants and clumps of sagebrush, but such sparse cover is not enough.

Yip! Yip! Yip! A prairie dog barks out the alarm call. Yip! Yap! Yip! Other dogs relay the danger before frantically diving below ground.

Coyote chases a prairie dog, but it escapes down a burrow. She retreats behind a small hill downwind. Her mate, also defeated in the hunt, lies down by her side. While they rest and wait, coyote thinks of her hungry pups.

Finally, three prairie dogs pop their heads above ground. They sniff the air and tilt their heads to the sky.

Yipper! Yapper! Yipeee! They bark out the all-is-safe signal. But coyote eyes are watching from behind the rocks.

Coyote and her mate lunge forward. Prairie dogs scramble for their burrows. This time, coyote digs frantically after a prairie dog while her mate lies motionless by another hole that may be the backdoor entrance to the same tunnel.

Panicked by coyote's digging, a prairie dog runs out the tunnel and straight into the jaws of coyote's mate. Snap! He gobbles it down.

Coyote takes a turn lying by a burrow backdoor, while her mate digs, dirt flying. Snap, snap! She catches her own prairie dog meal.

But now the prairie dogs are all safely hiding. The coyotes must look elsewhere for more food to take home to their hungry pups.

As the sun dips below the horizon, the coyotes lope across the prairie. Finally, they spot jackrabbit's ears, hidden in the evening shadows behind yucca spikes. Coyote sneaks closer from the south as her mate rushes in from the north. Jackrabbit leaps and runs, but is not fast enough to escape this time.

Coyote and her mate devour jackrabbit before trotting home under the rising moon. Their pups greet them with excited barks as the adults regurgitate food for them.

After the pups finish dinner, the coyote family sits outside the den. Coyote and her mate raise their noses and howl into the prairie night, while their pups imitate them and yip at the stars.

Before the night is over, coyote and her mate will leave the den again to hunt in the moonlight.

***

Nancy Dawson *loves the open landscapes and sweeping skies of the West. She lives and writes in Boulder, Colorado, and goes for hikes out her front door in the foothills of the Rocky Mountains.*

Goldfinches

Cynthia Pederson

Dandelion-gold,

finches dot the lawn like weeds—

eating ripe, white seeds.

Cynthia Pederson *lives between farm fence rows and walks through the once-prairie, loess hills of rural northwest Missouri.*

Bringing Back the Buffalo

GRETCHEN WOELFLE

More than a century has gone by since buffalo roamed the prairie by the millions. Their near extinction by the late 1800s meant a loss of wilderness for some people. For Lakota Indians it meant the loss of their traditional culture. Today, as the buffalo return, they are helping to revive that culture and to restore a healthy prairie ecosystem.

Grasses, growing two or three feet tall, roll over the hills of central South Dakota until they meet the Missouri River. A few shrubs and berry bushes break through the waves of grass. Ash, willow, and cottonwood trees line the river. This is mixed-grass prairie—not as tall as the tallgrass prairie to the east, taller than the sparse shortgrass prairie farther west. Dark figures move steadily across the landscape. Hundreds of buffalo—bulls, cows, and calves—graze to the edge of the Missouri River.

Fred DuBray oversees the fifteen hundred tribal buffalo that live on these forty thousand acres of Lakota reservation land. "It's the most beautiful land—and the best buffalo grazing land—in the world," brags DuBray. He is a member of the Lakota tribe, which is sometimes called the Cheyenne River Sioux.

Fred grew up here, but he didn't see a buffalo until he was fourteen, when his family traveled to Badlands National Park.

"I thought they were awesome," he says. He and his friends talked about bringing buffalo back, but they never thought it could really happen.

"When I was growing up, there was not a lot happening on the reservation," Fred remembers. "Many people felt helpless and hopeless. They felt cheated, like the buffalo had been."

In college, DuBray formed a plan to return the buffalo to his tribe. "People thought I was crazy, but I knew it was the only thing that would work. It was our last hope as a people."

As a tribal planner, DuBray talked about his buffalo plan to many of the ten thousand people living on the reservation. "Everyone got excited about the idea, but many of the older people were scared. They asked me, 'What if we're successful? When we had large healthy herds of buffalo, life was good. Then the army came and destroyed all that. What is to keep that from happening again?'"

Today, with fifteen hundred tribe-owned buffalo grazing on Lakota land, the fear fades as people reconnect with the buffalo.

King of the Prairie

The ancestors of these buffalo roamed the prairie for nearly ten thousand years. About fifty million pronghorn, American elk, and deer provided food for American Indian people. But the buffalo reigned as king of the prairie. About sixty million of these great beasts roamed the land before white settlers arrived. The buffalo gave people food, clothing, shelter, and tools. American Indians thought the buffalo was the greatest blessing the Great Spirit had given them. They believed that buffalo were their brothers and sisters.

Lame Deer, a Lakota medicine man living today, says, "You can't understand about nature, about the feeling we have for it, unless you understand how close we were to the buffalo. That animal was almost like a part of ourselves, part of our souls."

The Lakota based their social structure on the structure of the buffalo herd. DuBray says, "We learned how to live from them. During the summer, the buffalo herds used to break up into smaller herds. Then in the autumn they came together in the Black Hills [South Dakota] and spent the winter together. Our people did the same. Smaller family units would scatter in the summer, then meet and band together in a winter camp. We would hunt buffalo during the winter."

The Sun Dance, a famous Lakota religious ceremony, took place when the people came together again. It was done to gather energy to solve various problems and to pray for a good buffalo hunt.

All these connections broke down when the buffalo herds were destroyed. Fred DuBray explains, "The physical presence of the buffalo is the basis of our spiritual connection to the animals. When the buffalo were gone, our spiritual leaders had a tough time maintaining that connection."

Killing Off the Buffalo

In the 1840s the mass killing of the buffalo began—first by hunters who sold the hides and meat, then by travelers on trains who shot them for sport and left the carcasses to rot. By 1883 the herds were gone, and the U.S. Army forced starving American Indians, deprived of their food and way of life, to live on reservations.

But in 1894 a small herd of twenty-five buffalo was discovered deep in the wilderness of Yellowstone. Some ranchers, and the Bronx Zoo in New York City, had saved a few more. Congress passed a law protecting these animals in 1894, and buffalo are no longer a threatened species.

Today there are about two hundred thousand buffalo in the United States. That isn't many compared to the sixty million that once roamed the prairie, but it's a lot more than the six hundred that escaped the mass extinction one hundred years ago.

The Buffalo Return

No one is more committed to the return of the buffalo than American Indians. The InterTribal Bison Cooperative, founded by Fred DuBray in 1990, includes dozens of tribes that share information and resources.

Some tribes encourage traditional arts and crafts using buffalo leather and other products. All the tribes use the buffalo for food. DuBray says, "Our people have ten times as much heart disease and diabetes due to the high-fat diet of the mainstream American culture." Buffalo meat tastes a lot like beef but contains more protein and less fat. It is served at tribal pow-wows and in Head Start programs and is sold in local grocery stores. Many American Indians believe that eating beef makes them weak, but eating buffalo makes them strong.

The slaughter of the buffalo is itself a spiritual activity. A state-of-the-art processing machine was designed and built in Sweden for the Lakota tribe. Two large semitrailers enclose a stainless steel facility with full health and safety features. It contains equipment for pulling a hide, washing, and sterilizing, as well as coolers and generators. It also provides respect for the buffalo. Ceremonies and prayers are conducted before a buffalo is killed, and the processing plant is brought to the herd on the prairie. A buffalo is not forced into a slaughterhouse.

"We want to prove that business doesn't have to ruin the

environment or abuse the animals," says DuBray. "It can be ecological, spiritual, and make a profit."

For the Lakota, spiritual, cultural, and economic concerns were never separate. DuBray explains, "We concentrate on our spiritual relationship with the buffalo. This is the most important issue, but economics, society, and politics are a part of it. We believe that by treating the buffalo—and the earth—with the utmost respect, we will get the most economic benefit. We want to bring the outside world to that same understanding."

Fred DuBray has worked with the Lakota buffalo herd for ten years. "The buffalo is a very powerful animal. I enjoy being around powerful things. I hope the power will rub off on me, and it does."

Restoring the Prairie

Buffalo can help to restore the prairie ecosystem too. Some ecologists believe that cattle and prairie don't mix. They say the North European breeds of cattle that most ranchers raise degrade the land and the water sources.

But buffalo belong on the prairie. They thrived there for ten thousand years and the prairie thrived with them. Buffalo live on the grasses and forbs that grow there. They fertilize the soil. Their hooves force seeds deep in the earth.

Buffalo can survive scorching summers and harsh winters. When the frigid winter wind blows they turn directly into it and their thick fur coats keep them from freezing. They shake their huge heads and brush away the snow to find grass.

Buffalo resist most diseases and give birth easily on the prairie. They drink about once a day, but can go several days without water. They like to graze while they walk, traveling about four to five miles an hour. This roaming helps prevent overgrazing on the grassland.

Buffalo on the Ranch

Some non-Indian ranchers have begun raising buffalo. Their animals are not injected with hormones or antibiotics, as cattle are. But in some ways these ranch buffalo are treated just like cattle. When the buffalo are about eighteen months old, unwanted bulls or cows are sent to a feedlot, then to the slaughterhouse.

A feedlot is a crowded fenced area where the buffalo are fed grain for a few months to fatten them up before slaughter. But buffalo don't fatten up the way cattle do. Living in close quarters spreads disease and parasites that don't affect buffalo on the open range. Bison hate being confined. When they are not allowed to roam, they tend to fight and gore each other, so they are dehorned.

The Lakota system of buffalo management is no management—no feedlots, no vaccinations, no dehorning, no grain feeding. They let the buffalo live as wild animals.

Fred DuBray says, "When buffalo are intensely managed, their social structure is broken up. When you take the young calves away, wean them, and keep them separated from the older bunch, they never learn what it is to be a buffalo. They have instincts, but some of being a buffalo is learned behavior, just like us.

"One of our elders told me that if you're going to bring these buffalo back, first you have to ask the buffalo if they even want to come back. I don't think they would want to come back if they have to stand around in a feedlot. On the other hand, if they get to be buffalo and do what buffalo do, then I'm sure they would want to come back."

Teaching Children about Buffalo

The Lakota want to create a national park with their wild buffalo herds, east of Eagle Butte, South Dakota. "Our hope is that every person in this country will experience buffalo in the wild. It will help put our whole country back on track," claims Fred DuBray.

Lakota history traditionally has been recorded in their songs and dances. When the buffalo herds were destroyed, the buffalo disappeared from their songs and dances. Today, Lakota people again dance and sing about the buffalo.

Lakota children on the Cheyenne River Reservation know their buffalo herds well. They take school field trips to the animals. They hear classroom talks, witness the ceremonies before a killing, and eat buffalo meat. In the proposed national park, youth camps will allow young people to work with the herds.

Fred DuBray says, "American Indian children can relate deeply to the native species of their land. When you expose them to the buffalo, their instinctive knowledge is triggered. The buffalo are our university, and the entire prairie ecosystem is our campus."

Gretchen Woelfle *lives in Venice, California, and writes stories and environmental nonfiction for children.*

Comic Owl

ANN COOPER

Burrowing owls
in a prairie dog hole
tiny trolls of the dog town
like yo-yos   up   down
in a comic-*owl* dance—
feathery, freckled, eyes staring.

Burrowing owls
young chicks on a mound
looking around, so wary,
heads tilting, heads turning
three lanky-shanked fuzz balls
hearing the neighborhood warning

yip yip   yip yip
a prairie dog tips back
its head in alarm.
And gone in a flash—
not a sound, just a blur—
three young owls disappear.

Ann Cooper, *past "Brit" and present ardent Coloradoan, is a teacher-on-the-trail and has written ten nature books for children. Her poetry and stories for children have appeared in several magazines, including* Spider, Ladybug, R-A-D-A-R, Friend, *and* Clubhouse.

Prairie Spirits on the Wing

MARYBETH LORBIECKI

Many of us have a favorite animal from our region. But sometimes a favorite animal becomes something even more: a kindred spirit, and an inspiration.

My kindred spirit happens to be a bird. A golden throated, lyrical songster. It's not something I ever looked for, or expected. It just kind of happened.

I grew up in a city in the waistband of Minnesota, flat country that boasted granite under the belt and fertile fields as its everyday dress. In town, houses lay across the plains like dotted Swiss, and trees decorated the lines of its rivers, the Mississippi and the Sauk, giving the cityscape its shape.

I knew nothing about the history of the place except that this was my mom's hometown, and she had been a homecoming queen. Not much to go on. Also, about a mile from us, past the big Fingerhut Factory on Eighth Street, was a sign that you could read on your way into town over the Sauk bridge: ST. CLOUD, ALL-AMERICAN CITY, POP. 42,000.

I lived in a neighborhood of crackerbox bungalows with green Lego-block lawns. Once I'd reached the age of street crossing, I found my stomping ground as exciting as stale saltines. I wanted to EXPLORE, to find new lands, to discover new creatures, WILD creatures. So whenever Mom would let me, I'd follow my older brother, Mark, on my bike three blocks to the open fields behind the new North Junior High. There we'd stash the bikes and head out. The tall grasses burred our socks and swished our legs as we waded through. This was our wilderness.

Rumpled with little hummocks that I thought had to be prairie dog holes (Mark said they were just gopher holes), it rolled out before us, a mix of sweet cloverlike smells wafting up as we walked. I'd grab old woody stalks and point them at Mark like swords, or run and chase the monarchs, or collect striped caterpillars in my shirt pocket. I found flat stones I was sure were Indian arrowheads (Mark said they were just rocks) and gouges in the earth that had to be dinosaur footprints (Mark said they were just dried puddles). Plenty of other treasures caught my attention, too: box turtles and frogs, garter snakes (I can still pick up a garter snake with ease!) and salamanders, grasshoppers and beetles. That's not to mention the *Archie* comics, old newspapers, and dirty magazines we found, and the stack of mismatched pieces of wood for a fort Mark and I commandeered. On any given day, we could be pioneer sodbusters, Indians hunting buffalo, spies, or Johnny Quest and his enemy.

Our land of adventure stretched all the way from the busy street, Twelfth, to the Sauk River, the old broken-down Boy Scout bridge, and the airport. I loved tramping as far as that and then circling back for our bikes, then on through the vacant lots on the other side of Twenty-fifth Avenue. I knew nothing of the plants that I passed as we walked. To me, they were all weeds, but interesting ones—some with thorns to avoid and others with flowers to collect for Mom.

Though this was our wilderness, it wasn't our home.

Always keeping an eye out from different points in the fields were the stout, tenacious little stalk-hangers, the western meadowlarks. This was *their* territory, and the meadowlarks would make that clear, singing their national anthems in floating flutelike warbles. Perched on a swaying stalk of grass, white backs cloaked with a spattering of mud brown, each would proudly display its gilded throat and belly adorned by the shiny black V necklace. I thought they were great—troubadours for a queen (Mark said they were just meadowlarks).

But as impressive as each robed musician was to me, the bird really was a mere commoner. There were too many of them around to merit much attention (spotting a cardinal could give you points, but a meadowlark rated somewhere between a robin and a field sparrow).

As I grew, my wilderness changed. Houses rose up like baking cupcakes; first there was a scoop, a darkened mound, and then, pop, a whole house would appear, bare earth all around that would soon be frosted over in a shade of Astroturf. Soon followed the sidewalks and the cul-de-sacs, the community center and the ball fields, the churches and convenience stores. Each time a new building sprouted, my world shrank, the edges getting thicker and tighter until not a single undeveloped lot remained.

That's when I started wondering where the meadowlarks went. I also realized I suffer from an odd breed of claustrophobia—not of small inside places, but of small outside ones. In order to breathe properly, I discovered I need some unmade areas in the landscape around me—wooded ravines, abandoned railroad beds, wild edges of fields, unmowed meadows, or untethered grassy slopes, undocked beaches, untamed bluffs.

I've heard that when the Navajo make blankets, they

deliberately weave in a mistake or an empty spot, an opening in the pattern so that spirit is not locked in, but can flow in and out. Whether that's true or not, I seem to seek out places to live where there are one or two undeveloped spots, spaces that are not empty and not full, places in the middle, doorways for the spirit.

After I went away to college in the Twin Cities, I stopped visiting vacant lots, pastures, farm fields. And I stopped seeing meadowlarks. At first, I didn't miss them. I had my bits of wilderness in the woods on campus.

But when I traveled, my eyes would naturally scan the land, seeking out my sunshine-breasted friend. I'd never see one. At least not up close. The few I'd manage to spy were always on a fence post or an electric line as I rushed past in a car on the highway. I never got to *hear* one. It was like seeing a silent movie with no subtitles or musical score. And my imagination had no hope of creating anything like a meadowlark's melody.

I knew that the fewer prairies and open lots there were, the fewer the meadowlarks. But now rumor had it that birds were up against technology. New farm machinery had made it possible to plant earlier in the spring and harvest earlier in the fall. This meant fields swept clean first of nests and later of the plumping-up food required for the meadowlarks' autumn migration. More and more of the birds weren't making it. Perilous stuff.

Then I took a trip to Nebraska. On a short trek at dawn, I was greeted by a dazzling, yellow-throated, black-spangled male atop a fence post only three yards from me. He tossed back his beak and sang as if performing for only me. Such incredible dips and trills! He went on and on for a full ten-minute performance. He even drew a crowd of six, standing around him awed, and rather than being frightened, that meadowlark puffed himself up like an opera star and sang all the harder, his throat wobbling like a grasshopper was jumping up and down in there. He was the cockiest, most handsome bird I had ever met. I was enchanted. I was in love. Just what he wanted.

But I am fickle, and I could not sit there all day. So I eventually got in my car and drove away.

I did not forget him, though. I had caught his song on a little tape recorder I had brought along for interviews. The tape could not do him justice.

Not long afterward, I asked my husband, David, to design a logo for my freelance writing business. I thought he would create something that made you think of ink and paper and books. That's when fate stepped up for notice. The logo David unveiled was a meadowlark crafted in black ink, like an old-fashioned woodcarving, with my name linked to it in space. The bird's head was tipped and its tail long and fanned, like that of a mythic bird set to carry me away with song—my siren. Startled, I asked, "Why a meadowlark?"

David shrugged. "It seemed right."

And it did. I looked at that little guy on my calling card and knew why we had been paired. We both loved the same kinds of spaces, the out-of-the-way spots, far from the crowds, filled with tall grasses and bordered by trees. We didn't quite fit in the run-of-the-mill places, and we didn't want to talk, we wanted to sing—to do things our own way and do it with flourish!

A little while later, it became clear that all this stuff about loving wild lands and having a kindred spirit was not a free ride. My family and I had moved to Wisconsin, and I was asked to help work on a project to preserve twenty thousand acres of prairies and grassland in Polk and St. Croix Counties. Our goal? To save these spots for the future and protect the disappearing prairie and grassland wildlife species whose habitats were being built or paved over. Guess who was one of these species? The western meadowlark, of course. Its population had declined 90 percent in thirty years.

Almost as if touched by a charm, I was transformed into the president of a citizens' group, the Western Wisconsin Prairie Project.

And who did I start seeing (more than anyone else did, I'm

sure) on power lines and country fence posts? My friend the meadowlark, calling away at me, cajoling, reminding, beseeching. In fact, I was beginning to find him a bit of a nag, since this citizens' group was no easy deal: meetings, phone calls, letters, presentations, brochures, contests.

Of necessity, the summer transformed into a crash course on the meadowlark's original home—the prairies. My spirit bird was presenting to me a cornucopia of delights: purple wands of blazing stars, yellow sparks of partridge peas, nodding round faces of bright sunflowers, winking blue-eyed grasses, crimson torches of cardinal flowers, and the majestic grasses turning rippling shades of blue, purple, rust, and wheat in autumn's crisper.

Having made the acquaintance of some of the prairie's flowers and plants, and their beauty, the richness of my early wilderness hit me in a new way. I wished I could go back in time and walk those fields behind North Junior High again, just for the thrill of it (especially with my brother, Mark, so this time he could be the tagalong and I could be the smart aleck). Had those furrowless fields been prairie remnants? I wished I knew. I wished, too, that I could zip even further backward in a time machine to see the past life of my first wilderness, the wildlife and the peoples who had come before me, the Sauk, the Dakota, the Ojibwa, the voyageurs and the settlers.

Since I can't live in reverse, though, I've started reading a little area history and planting prairie species in every blank spot in my world: front yard, back yard, side yard, boulevard—a new obsession from my feathered sidekick. And I've cheered from the sidelines as some kids in Clear Lake, Wisconsin, cleaned up the abandoned, littered land behind their school and planted a new prairie future, one complete with meadowlarks, we hope.

As for my project, the governor of Wisconsin recently signed the Western Wisconsin Prairie Habitat Restoration Area into reality. Over the coming years, the state will make partnerships with landowners, land trusts, parks, and others to make permanent homes for the meadowlark and the other grasslands wildlife in our area. My two young prairie-loving daughters, Nadja and Mirjana, frontline workers on the project, each received one of the governor's commemorative pens. I hope they will always remember the parts they played in putting aside some grassy spirit holes for our prairie pals. Perhaps they'll even find that one of those birds or butterflies or frogs or snakes picks them to be their kindred spirit.

As for my kindred spirit, it flies on before me, resting on fence posts and singing till I catch up. Looks like I'm in for a lifetime of prairie adventures, whether I'm ready for them or not.

~

Marybeth Lorbiecki *loves the outdoors and writing about it for kids and adults. She has won awards for her Earthwise Books and biographies of the conservationist Aldo Leopold—*Of Things Natural, Wild, and Free *(for youth) and* Aldo Leopold: A Fierce Green Fire *(for young adults and adults). Her most recent book is about the relationship of the Dakota (Sioux) to the land and a man who painted them in the 1830s and 1840s—*Painting the Dakota: Seth Eastman at Fort Snelling. *She lives in Hudson, Wisconsin, with her husband, David, and three birdwatching, prairie-loving, canoeing children: Nadja, Mirjana, and Dmitri.*

Appendixes

Ecology of the Great North American Prairie

What Is an Ecoregion?

The *Stories from Where We Live* series celebrates the literature of North America's diverse *ecoregions*. Ecoregions are large geographic areas that share similar climate, soils, and plant and animal communities. Thinking ecoregionally helps us understand how neighboring cities and states are connected, and makes it easier for people to coordinate the use and protection of shared rivers, forests, watersheds, mountain ranges, and other natural areas. For our part, we believe that ecoregions provide an illuminating way to organize and compare place-based literature.

While many institutions have mapped the world's ecoregions, no existing delineation of ecoregions (or similar unit, such as *provinces* or *bioregions*) proved perfectly suited to a literary series. We created our own set of ecoregions based largely on existing scientific designations, with an added consideration for regional differences in human culture.

THE

NORTHWEST

PACIFIC

COAST

BOREAL

GREAT

NORT

ROCKY MOUNTAINS

CALIFORNIA

COAST

WESTERN

DESERTS

AND

PLATEAUS

HAWAIIAN
ISLANDS

ARCTIC

FOREST

NORTHEAST
WOODLANDS

NORTH

ATLANTIC

COAST

GREAT LAKES

AMERICAN

PRAIRIE

APPALACHIAN
HIGHLANDS

SOUTH
ATLANTIC
COAST
AND
PIEDMONT

SOUTHERN
HILL
COUNTRY

GULF COAST

Defining the Great North American Prairie

Most of the time when people talk about "prairie," they're referring to a particular natural community defined by low rainfall, hardy grasses, a scarcity of trees, and a particular pack of critters—such as pronghorn and prairie dogs, lark buntings and bobolinks. Our Great North American Prairie ecoregion is, quite simply, the area on this continent that was once dominated by those prairie communities. It's a huge region, extending from the eastern edge of the Rocky Mountains all the way to Illinois, and from Alberta and Saskatchewan south to western Texas.

For the record, stretches of prairie do exist in other parts of North America, such as northern Indiana and southern Michigan. But our ecoregion is a single geographic unit, and for this reason it doesn't include these scattered "islands" of prairie.

Once a continuous sea of grass, the Great North American Prairie now consists largely of ranches and farms that grow timothy and wheat instead of buffalo grass and bluestem. Modern cities now stand on the sites of early Indian villages, and highways crisscross the plains where deer trails and wagon roads once lay.

But for all these changes, this is still the prairie. Dig beneath the asphalt and you'll find deep, fertile soils. Spend a year here and you'll experience dizzying extremes of weather: hot, dry summers; woolly winters; and always the wild west wind. Poke through roadside weeds and you may still find fringed orchids and prairie clover. Visit wilder corners, and prairie chickens, coyotes, and jackrabbits may scurry across your path.

What's more, the people who live here have been shaped in many ways by the prairie environment. The stories of the Great North American Prairie reflect some of the commonalities of this culture: the ways people respond to the great spread of sky and land, their fortitude in the face of dramatic weather, and the ways they have created community and connectedness in a vast and often sparsely populated place.

Habitats

If you could travel back in time a million years, you'd discover that the region now known as the Great North American Prairie was once covered with a huge tropical rain forest. When did the trees disappear? When did the grass take over?

Scientists say that large-scale climate changes made the region drier and caused the tropical forest to recede. The emergence of the Rocky Mountains helped dry things out, too. Rising up out of the flat plains, the Rockies forced air masses from the west up to higher, colder elevations where they condensed and squeezed out their moisture as rain or snow. By the time the clouds descended down the Rockies' eastern slopes, they were all but dry. The pattern remains to this day, and helps explain the three basic zones of the prairie. Bordering the Rockies is the most arid of the trio, the shortgrass prairie, which receives only about ten inches of rain a year. Two hundred miles to the east, rainfall increases to about twenty inches a year and the taller, mixed-grass prairie begins. Another two hundred miles east, annual rainfall averages about thirty inches, and the result is the comparatively lush tallgrass prairie.

Once grasses took hold on the prairie, other factors conspired to keep trees out. The tangle of growth above and below ground made it hard for tree seeds to settle in the soil. Grazing bison, elk, and pronghorn pruned back vegetation as they ranged within the region, and it was easier for grasses to bounce back than it was for trees. In addition, fires raged throughout the prairie on a regular basis, which also favored grasses since most of their growth lies safely underground.

Anyone who lives on the prairie today knows that it's hardly a monotonous grassland, though. High buttes, badlands, and other geologic formations punctuate the landscape. And in addition to the three distinct zones mentioned above, a number of other habitats add variety to the terrain. A *habitat* is the particular type of place where a creature finds the food, shelter, and space it needs to thrive. The following sections highlight some of the dominant wildlife habitats of the Great North American Prairie ecoregion, and describe some of the plants and animals that live there.

Shortgrass Prairie: Life on the shortgrass prairie, or High Plains, isn't easy. The wind laps up much of the moisture that falls, hail storms batter the land, and the short buffalo grass and blue grama grass that dominate the region offer little protection from the elements. Nonetheless, many creatures have adapted well to life on the High Plains—so well, in fact, that some would have a harder time living on less exposed terrain. For example, speedy runners, such as pronghorn, swift fox, and jackrabbits, rely on wide-open spaces to outdistance their pursuers.

Many High Plains creatures find it advantageous to live in groups. Consider the prairie dog town, a marvel of animal interdependence. Burrowing owls, jackrabbits, kangaroo rats, toads, snakes, box turtles, and spiders pop into prairie dog tunnels for temporary shelter much like people duck into their neighbors' storm cellars to escape rough weather. Some animals even live there permanently. Above ground, elk and bison like to nibble the new growth around the prairie dog towns; similarly, prairie dogs often build their towns where bison and elk have heavily grazed so that they can have a clear view of terrestrial predators. Harvester ants build their hills on top of prairie dog mounds. Black-footed ferrets, the most endangered mammals in North America, live only where there are ample prairie dogs to eat. The bare earth around prairie dog towns even makes a perfect dance floor for prairie chickens to come strut their stuff each spring!

Much of the High Plains is now used for ranching, but about 60 percent of the region still remains in grass. (Examples: "Springtime on the Plains"; "Salamander"; "Coyote Hunts.")

Mixed-Grass Prairie: Lying between the High Plains and the tallgrass prairie is the mixed-grass prairie. These days the region is dominated by crops, including wheat, barley, soybeans, and flax. But where native prairie grasses grow, you can find a great diversity of plants and animals. Little bluestem is the most common grass of this region, but you'll also find short grasses from the High Plains sprouting up beside wildflowers and patches of tall grass from the East. Pronghorn, prairie dogs, and swift fox reach their eastern limit here, overlapping with eastern cottontails, eastern moles, and least shrews from the East.

It was here on the vast mixed-grass prairie that bison once roamed in greatest number. According to scientists' best estimates, as many as sixty million may have thundered over these great plains. Although bison numbered less than one thousand by 1900, as many as two hundred thousand once again graze and gallop on the Great North American Prairie. Their return reflects the growing interest in restoring the mixed-grass prairie, and the hard work of prairie conservationists and innovative ranchers. (Examples: "The Country of Grass"; "Going Home to Nicodemus"; "Bringing Back the Buffalo.")

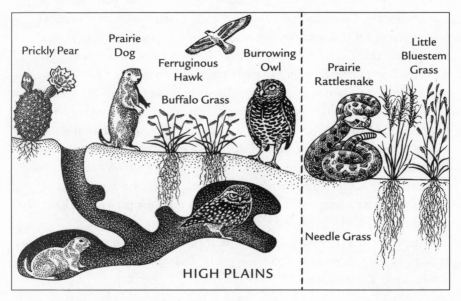

Prickly Pear · Prairie Dog · Ferruginous Hawk · Buffalo Grass · Burrowing Owl · Prairie Rattlesnake · Little Bluestem Grass · Needle Grass

HIGH PLAINS

0 to 200 miles east of the Rocky Mountains   200 to 400 miles

Tallgrass Prairie: Grasses more than ten feet high and a dazzling array of wildflowers make the tallgrass prairie a striking landscape. Its rich soil proved irresistible to early settlers, who plowed under much of the original prairie to make way for their own favorite tall grass: corn. Still you can find remnants of the tall grass in prairie preserves, railway borders, cemeteries, and other parts of the Midwest. In fact, the Flint Hills of Kansas contain almost three million acres of mostly undisturbed tallgrass prairie.

Animals of the tallgrass prairie have adapted to the scarcity of trees in all sorts of ways. Like its cousin the prairie dog, the pocket gopher of the tallgrass prairie opts to burrow. In fact, pocket gophers almost never come above ground. Instead, they spend most of their time in vast networks of tunnels that include separate rooms for eating, sleeping, and defecating.

Birds, too, have adapted to the treeless terrain. More than half of all prairie birds nest on the ground. Unlike forest birds, which sing from a perch, most prairie birds, including lark sparrows, bobolinks, and meadowlarks, sing while flying! The songs of prairie birds even carry

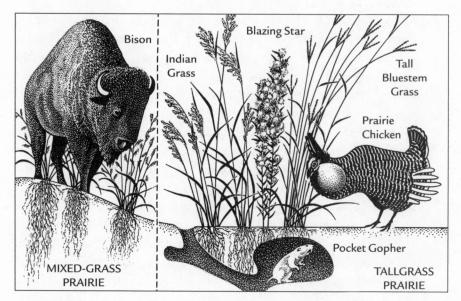

east of the Rockies   400+ miles east of the Rockies

farther than those of forest birds. So if you find a patch of tallgrass prairie during the spring or summer months, you're bound to enjoy great sights *and* great sounds. (Examples: "Big Grass"; "Fire Crazy"; "Corn"; "Prairie Spirits on the Wing.")

Prairie Potholes: For thousands of years, North America's waterfowl have owed their survival to "prairie potholes"—small- to medium-sized ponds that lie scattered across the dry northern plains. Formed by melted chunks of ice that gouged into the ground during the last glaciation, prairie potholes once numbered in the millions. Many potholes have since been drained for farming, but those that remain sustain thousands of migrating snow geese, sandhill cranes, ducks, and more. Each spring, the potholes fill up with rain and melted snow, becoming nature's version of a giant birdbath. Surrounding grasses offer safe shelter and nest sites. Fish, insects, and amphibians provide ample food. Together these conditions make the prairie potholes among the most important habitats for migratory and nesting birds in all of North America! (Example: "Migration Prayer: The Geese Speak.")

Rivers, Marshes, Sloughs: The rivers of the prairie region have played a big role in the human history of the region. They've eased travel, speeded commerce, produced power, and provided water for thirsty mouths and thirsty crops. But they have also shaped and sustained the prairie's natural communities. Narrow forests of willows, cottonwoods, and shrubs often line the region's rivers, attracting forest songbirds and other animals that would not be able to live on the open plains. Periodic flooding of the rivers creates marshes, sloughs, and other nutrient-filled wetlands where herons, frogs, turtles, and other aquatic creatures gather. Flocks of migrating birds follow the Mississippi River north and south each spring and fall, and others stop to rest on the broad, shallow sections of the Platte.

Human activity has significantly altered many stretches of rivers in the Great North American Prairie. Dams designed to maintain water supplies during the dry months turn shallow, bird-friendly rivers into deep lakes. Highways laid out to follow the river's curves end up creating a lot of traffic noise that can disturb river-loving wildlife. All around the prairie, though, people are trying to rethink these practices to better balance the needs of people *and* wildlife. (Examples: "The Last Best Swimming Hole"; "River Dance.")

Cities and Suburbs: As soon as settlers established homesteads on the Great North American Prairie, they began changing the landscape around them. They replaced native grasses with their crops. They suppressed wildfires to keep their crops and towns from burning. They planted flowers and trees from the East to fill their yards with familiar sights and to protect their homes from wind and sun.

Not surprisingly, then, the towns and cities of the Great North American Prairie contain many of the same species found in urbanized parts of the rest of the country. You'll find Norway maples, elms, and other non-native trees growing alongside typical prairie species. You'll see plenty of squirrels, raccoons, and other city-tolerant animals. But sometimes the variety of wildlife in urbanized areas will surprise you: in the spring and fall, for example, you may be able to spot an incredible diversity of migrating songbirds pausing to rest in prairie communities.

In hopes of supporting more regional species, some prairie residents have decided to restore native vegetation in their yards and communities. In this way, they often save on the water and energy required to grow non-native species, and they invite rare butterflies, birds, and small mammals into close viewing range. (Examples: "Midway Morning"; "Snow Print Two: Hieroglyphics"; "Goldfinches.")

Animals and Plants

Here's a brief rundown of the animals and plants of the Great North American Prairie mentioned in the literature of this anthology.

Birds: Perching birds of the prairie include meadowlarks, horned larks, lark buntings, bobolinks, field sparrows, red-winged blackbirds, American robins, jays, gold-finches, common grackles, cardinals, American crows, orioles, kingbirds, magpies, and common ravens. Among the *fowl-like birds* that stay closer to the ground are ring-necked pheasants and prairie chickens.

Lark Sparrow

Long-legged wading birds, such as sandhill cranes, whooping cranes, and herons, share prairie waterways with *ducklike birds* (for example, Canada geese and snow geese) and *small wading birds,* including upland plovers, mountain plovers, and killdeer. Among the many *birds of prey* on the prairie are red-tailed hawks, eagles, and burrowing owls (also called billy owls).

Sandhill
Crane

Mammals: The prairie is home to a number of large mammals, including bison (also called buffalo), elk, pronghorn (also called antelope), and deer (mule and white-tailed), and coyotes (which have sometimes been called prairie wolves). In addition, you can find many medium- and small-sized mammals, including prairie dogs, gophers, weasels, badgers, ground squirrels, wood-chucks, jackrabbits, kit foxes, muskrats, skunks, bats, chipmunks, cottontail rabbits, squirrels, deer mice, and field mice.

Pronghorn

Grasshopper

Invertebrates (all insects): Grasshoppers, moths, formaldehyde ants, dragonflies, ladybugs, tumble-bugs (or dung beetles), and monarch butterflies are among the prairie insects named in this anthology. But don't let this short list fool you: in the summer, as many as ten million insects may be inhabiting an acre of tall-grass prairie. And their variety is as great as the colorful grasses and flowers they pollinate and feed on.

Fish: Many freshwater fish swim through the prairie's lakes, rivers, and streams. Chubs and minnows are two fish mentioned in this volume.

Reptiles and Amphibians: Common prairie *reptiles* include rattle-snakes, bull snakes, garter snakes, horned toads (really a lizard), and box turtles. Among the many *amphibi-ans* here are frogs and salamanders.

Tiger Salamander

Plants: Trees and shrubs (including cacti) of the prairie region include cottonwoods, willows, aspens, maples, oaks, wild plum (or American plum), box elder, ash, Russian olive, lo-custs, raspberries, sage, sagebrush, snakeweed, wild prairie rose, button cactus, and prickly pear cactus. Prairie *wildflowers and grasses* include partridge pea, blazing star, pearly everlasting, black-eyed Susans, Philadelphia lilies, pasqueflower, asters, goats-beard, coneflowers, prairie rose hips, irises, white lady slippers, sunflowers, gentians, western prairie fringed orchids, goldenrod, gaillardia, buffalo bur, yucca, nettle, milkweed, thistle weed, skeleton weed, ragweed, wild turnips, wild sweet potatoes, wild onions, cardinal flowers, horseweed, tumbleweed, ground cherry, buffalo grass, big bluestem, little bluestem, Indian grass, side-oats grama, and blue grama. (Kochia is an introduced plant from Europe.)

Woodlily

Black-eyed Susans

Stories by State or Province

Colorado

1. "The Blizzard"
2. "Springtime on the Plains"
3. "Nature's Ways"
4. "Tumbleweeds"
5. "Coyote Hunts"
6. "Comic Owl"

Illinois

7. "Riding the Rails"
8. "Children of the Sun"

Iowa

9. "Corn"
10. "Reflections on Gullies"
11. "In the Autumn Grass"
12. "How to Replant a Prairie"

Kansas

13. "Outside Abilene"
14. "Tales from Tornado Alley"
15. "The Last Best Swimming Hole"
16. "Going Home to Nicodemus"
17. "Disappearances"

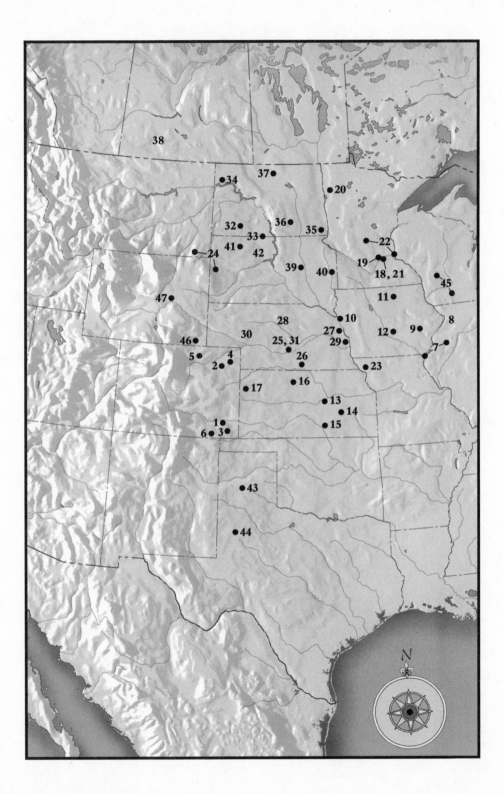

Minnesota

Missouri

Montana

Nebraska

North Dakota

Saskatchewan, Canada

Parks and Preserves

Listed below are just a few of the many places where you can go to experience the wilder side of the Great North American Prairie ecoregion. Bear in mind that some of these states straddle more than one ecoregion, so we have included only natural areas in the prairie region of the states. Also, please note that the phone numbers provided are sometimes for the park's headquarters, but often for a managing agency or organization. In any case, the people at these numbers can provide you with details about the area and directions for how to get there!

Alberta, Canada

Dinosaur Provincial Park (Patricia) 403-378-4342
Elk Island National Park (Fort Saskatchewan) 780-992-2950
Head-Smashed-In Buffalo Jump (Fort Macleod) 403-553-2731

Colorado

Adobe Creek Reservoir State Wildlife Area (Las Animas) 719-336-4852
Bonny Lake State Park/South Republican River State Wildlife Area (Idalia) 970-354-7306
Comanche National Grasslands (Springfield) 719-523-6591
Pawnee National Grassland (Greeley) 970-353-5004
Tamarack Ranch State Wildlife Area (Crook, Sterling) 970-842-3124

Illinois

Apple River Canyon State Park (Apple River) 815-745-3302
Ayres Sand Prairie Nature Preserve (Carroll County) 815-273-2731
Chautauqua and Emiquon National Wildlife Refuges (Havana) 309-535-2290

Hanover Bluff Nature Preserve (Hanover) 815-745-3302

Mark Twain National Wildlife Refuge Complex (Quincy) 217-224-8580

Mississippi Palisades State Park (Savanna) 815-273-2731

Nachusa Grasslands (Dixon) 815-456-2340

Revis Hill Prairie Nature Preserve (Mason County) 309-597-2212

Iowa

Broken Kettle Grasslands (Plymouth County) 515-244-5044

Cedar Hills Sand Prairie (Black Hawk County) 515-244-5044

Desoto National Wildlife Refuge (Missouri Valley) 712-642-4121

Driftless Area National Wildlife Refuge (McGregor) 319-873-3423

Effigy Mounds National Monument (Harpers Ferry) 319-873-3491

Greiner Family Nature Preserve (Muscatine County) 515-244-5044

Ledges State Park (Madrid) 515-432-1852

Neal Smith National Wildlife Refuge (Prairie City) 515-994-3400

Preparation Canyon State Park (Onawa) 712-423-2829

Union Slough National Wildlife Refuge (Titonka) 515-928-2523

Kansas

Cheyenne Bottoms Wildlife Area (Great Bend) 316-793-3066

Cimarron National Grassland (Elkhart) 316-697-4621

Finney Game Refuge (Garden City) 316-276-9400

Flint Hills National Wildlife Refuge (Hartford) 316-392-5553

Kirwin National Wildlife Refuge (Kirwin) 913-543-6673

Konza Prairie (Manhattan) 785-587-0441

Lake Scott State Park (Scott City) 316-872-2061

The Land Institute (Salina) 785-823-5376

Maxwell Wildlife Refuge (Canton) 316-628-4455

Quivira National Wildlife Refuge (Stafford) 316-486-2393

Minnesota

Big Stone National Wildlife Refuge (Odessa) 320-273-2191

Blue Mounds State Park (Luverne) 507-283-1307

Bluestem Prairie Scientific and Natural Area (Clay County)
218-498-2679

Chippewa Prairie (Milan) 612-331-0750

Frontenac State Park (Frontenac) 651-345-3401

Hole-in-the-Mountain Prairie (Lake Benton) 612-331-0750

Minnesota Valley National Wildlife Refuge (Bloomington)
952-854-5900

Pembina Trails Preserve (Polk County) 612-331-0750

Weaver Dunes Scientific and Natural Area (Wabasha County)
612-331-0750

Missouri

Brickyard Hill Loess Mound Prairie Natural Area (Atchison County)
816-271-3100

Marmaton River Bottoms Natural Area (Nevada) 314-968-1105

Osage Prairie Natural Area (Nevada) 417-395-2341

Pershing State Park (Laclede) 660-963-2299

Prairie State Park (Liberal) 417-843-6711

Squaw Creek National Wildlife Refuge (Mound City) 660-442-3187

Star School Hill Prairie Natural Area (Atchison County) 816-271-3100

Swan Lake National Wildlife Refuge (Sumner) 660-856-3323

Montana

Bowdoin National Wildlife Refuge (Malta) 406-654-2863

Hailstone National Wildlife Refuge (Rapelje) 406-538-8706

Makoshika State Park (Glendive) 406-365-6256

Medicine Rocks State Park (Ekalaka) 406-232-0900

Charles M. Russell National Wildlife Refuge (Lewistown)
406-538-8706

Nebraska

Crescent Lake National Wildlife Refuge (Scottsbluff) 308-635-7851

Fort Niobrara National Wildlife Refuge (Valentine) 402-376-3789

Fort Robinson State Park (Crawford) 308-665-2900

Nebraska National Forest (Chadron) 308-432-0300

Nine Mile Prairie (Lincoln) 402-472-2971
North Platte National Wildlife Refuge (Scottsbluff) 308-635-7851
Oglala National Grassland (Chadron) 308-432-4475
Rainwater Basin Wetland Management District (Kearney)
    308-236-5015
Samuel McKelvie National Forest (Nenzel) 402-823-4154
Scotts Bluff National Monument (Gering) 308-436-4340
Valentine National Wildlife Refuge (Valentine) 402-376-3789

North Dakota

Chase Lake National Wildlife Refuge (Woodworth) 701-752-4218
Cross Ranch Nature Preserve (Hensler) 701-222-8464
Des Lacs National Wildlife Refuge (Kenmare) 701-385-4046
Little Missouri State Park (Killdeer) 701-794-3731
Lostwood National Wildlife Refuge (Kenmare) 701-848-2722
J. Clark Salyer National Wildlife Refuge (Upham) 701-768-2548
Sheyenne National Grasslands (Lisbon) 701-683-4342
Smith Grove Wildlife Management Area (near Mandan) 701-328-6300
Theodore Roosevelt National Park (Medora) 701-623-4466
Upper Souris National Wildlife Refuge (Berthold) 701-468-5467

Saskatchewan, Canada

Buffalo Pound Provincial Park (Moose Jaw) 306-694-3659
Cypress Hills Interprovincial Park (Maple Creek) 306-662-4411
Douglas Provincial Park (Elbow) 306-854-2177
Grasslands National Park (Val Marie) 306-298-2257
Greenwater Lake Provincial Park (Porcupine Plain) 306-278-3516
Moose Mountain Provincial Park (Kenosee Lake) 306-577-2600

South Dakota

Badlands National Park (Interior) 605-433-5361
Black Hills National Forest (Custer) 605-673-2251
Buffalo Gap National Grassland (Hot Springs) 605-745-4107
Custer State Park (Custer) 605-255-4515
LaCreek National Wildlife Refuge (Martin) 605-685-6508

Lake Andes National Wildlife Refuge (Lake Andes) 605-487-7603
Samuel Ordway Prairie (Leola) 605-439-3475
Sand Lake National Wildlife Refuge (Columbia) 605-885-6320
Waubay National Wildlife Refuge (Waubay) 605-947-4521

Texas

Buffalo Lake National Wildlife Refuge (Umbarger) 806-499-3382
Caprock Canyons State Park (Quitaque) 806-455-1492
McClellan Creek National Grassland (Gray County) 405-497-2143
Muleshoe National Wildlife Refuge (Muleshoe) 806-946-3341
Rita Blanca National Grassland (Dallam County) 505-374-9652

Wisconsin

Avoca Prairie-Savanna State Natural Area (Avoca) 608-588-2591
Black River State Forest (Black River Falls) 715-284-4103
Necedah National Wildlife Refuge (Necedah) 608-565-2551
Perrot State Park (Trempealeau) 608-534-6409
Quincy Bluff and Wetlands Preserve (White Creek) 608-251-8140
Upper Mississippi River National Wildlife and Fish Refuge (La Crosse
    District: Onalaska) 608-783-8405
Wyalusing State Park (Bagley) 608-996-2261

Wyoming

Black Hills National Forest (eastern Wyoming and western South
    Dakota) 605-673-2251
Hutton Lake National Wildlife Refuge (Laramie) 970-723-8202
Keyhole State Park (Moorcroft) 307-756-3596
Sybille Wildlife Research and Education Center (Wheatland)
    307-322-2784
Thunder Basin National Grassland (Douglas) 307-358-4690

Recommended Reading

Brown, Lauren. *Grasslands*. (The Audubon Society Nature Guides.) New York: Alfred A. Knopf, Inc., 1985.

Cushman, Ruth Carol, and Stephen R. Jones. *The Shortgrass Prairie*. Boulder: Pruett Publishing Co., 1988.

Llamas, Andreu. *The Great Plains*. Broomall, Pa.: Chelsea House Publishers, 1996.

Madson, John. *Where the Sky Began: Land of the Tallgrass Prairie*. Boston: Houghton Mifflin, 1982.

Manning, Richard. *Grassland: The History, Biology, Politics and Promise of the American Prairie*. New York: Penguin USA, 1997.

Shepherd, Lansing. *The Northern Plains: Minnesota, North Dakota, South Dakota*. (The Smithsonian Guides to Natural America.) New York: Random House, 1996.

Staub, Frank. *America's Prairies*. Minneapolis: Carolrhoda Books, 1993.

Winckler, Suzanne. *The Heartland: Illinois, Iowa, Nebraska, Kansas, Missouri*. (The Smithsonian Guides to Natural America.) New York: Random House, 1997.

Special Thanks

I have always been fond of prairies. In fact, were it not for a certain bank of clouds that arrived at exactly three-thirty one October afternoon, I would have been married in one. When it came time to edit this anthology, though, I was living miles from the Midwest and from the nearest prairie. So I am extremely grateful for the thoughtful input of my many prairie-wise friends and colleagues.

First thanks go to Miriam Stewart, who lent me a number of great books, including Connie Mutel and Mary Swander's *Land of the Fragile Giants*. Second thanks go to Connie Mutel, who in turn helped me locate the authors in her book and other Iowa writing. Scott Semken of Ice Cube Press, Ann Cooper, and Mary Peace Finley of the Society of Children's Book Writers and Illustrators all hooked me up with literary networks in the prairie region. Luise Woelflein and Marybeth Lorbiecki helped me track down tornado tales. Ken Setterington of the Toronto Public Library recommended some of his favorite children's writers and stories from the Canadian prairie. And John Knott of the University of Michigan and Scott Russell Sanders of Indiana University both steered me toward some of the region's best nature writing.

Stephen R. Jones kindly reviewed several sections of this anthology for scientific accuracy. Any errors and oversights that remain are my own responsibility.

I owe enormous thanks to my loyal "teacher" team—Priscilla Howell, Jen Kretser, and Jen Lindstrom—for lending their time, talents, and humor to this project. Their commitment to children and to the natural world is an inspiration. And of course, thanks to Robin, for listening, critiquing, and reassuring, and for always knowing which to do when.

One of the real pleasures of editing these anthologies is that it gives rise to countless conversations with friends and family about my chosen region and its literature. So a final thank-you goes to all of you who reminisced with me about a favorite scene from Willa Cather or a beloved chapter from the *Little House* series, or who shared with me your own memories of the lands of the Great North American Prairie. Like the writings themselves, you made a few wintry months in Cambridge, Massachusetts, come alive with rippling bluestem and spacious skies.

Contributor Acknowledgments

Alurista, "cornfields thaw out," *Revista Chicano-Riqueña* 9, no. 1 (Winter 1981). Copyright © 1982 by Alurista. Reprinted with permission from the author.

Sanora Babb, "Nature's Ways," excerpted from *An Owl on Every Post* (New York: McCall Publishing Company, 1970), 111–17. Copyright © 1970 and renewed 1998 by Sanora Babb. Reprinted with permission from the author.

Julene Bair, "Disappearances," adapted from *One Degree West: Reflections of a Plainsdaughter* (Minneapolis: Mid-List Press, 2000), 1–17. Copyright © 2000 by Julene Bair. Reprinted with permission from Mid-List Press.

Art Bettis, excerpted from "Reflections on Gullies," in *Land of the Fragile Giants: Landscapes, Environments, and Peoples of the Loess Hills,* ed. Cornelia F. Mutel and Mary Swander (Iowa City: University of Iowa Press, 1994), 30–34. Copyright © 1994 by the University Museums, Iowa State University. Reprinted with permission from the University Museums and University of Iowa Press.

Hal Borland, "Springtime on the Plains," excerpted from *High, Wide and Lonesome* (Philadelphia: J. B. Lippincott and Company, 1956), 211–16. Copyright © 1956 by Hal Borland. Copyright renewed 1984 by Barbara Dodge Borland. Reprinted with permission from Frances Collin, Literary Agent.

Willa Cather, "The Country of Grass," excerpted from *My Ántonia* (Boston: Houghton Mifflin Company, 1918).

George Catlin, "Prairie Fire," excerpted from *Letters and Notes on the Manners, Customs, and Conditions of the North American Indians* (New York: Wiley and Putnam, 1841).

"Children of the Sun," from "The Omaha Tribe" by Alice C. Fletcher and Francis La Flesche in *Twenty-Seventh Annual Report of the Bureau of American*

Ethnology to the Secretary of the Smithsonian Instituiton. (Washington, D.C.: United States Government Printing Office, 1911), 63.

Daniel Chu and Bill Shaw, "Going Home to Nicodemus," excerpted from *Going Home to Nicodemus* (Morristown, N.J.: Julian Messner, 1994), 5–7, 35–38. Copyright © 1994 by Dan Chu and Associates. Reprinted with permission from Dan Chu and Associates.

Helen Colella, "A Poppin' Tale." Copyright © 2001 by Helen Colella. Printed with permission from the author.

Georgia Cook, "Raspberries," *Proceedings from the 124th Annual Conference of the Wisconsin Academy of Science, Arts, and Letters* (April 23, 1994), 33. Copyright © 1994 by Georgia Cook. Reprinted with permission from the author.

Ann Cooper, "Comic Owl" and "River Dance." Copyright © 2001 by Ann Cooper. Printed with permission from the author.

Nancy Dawson, "Coyote Hunts." Copyright © 2001 by Nancy Dawson. Printed with permission from the author.

Jan Donley, "Salamander." Copyright © 2001 by Jan Donley. Printed with permission from the author.

Douglas C. Dosson, "From Thin Air." Copyright © 2001 by Douglas C. Dosson. Printed with permission from the author.

Harley Elliott, "Outside Abilene," *Minnesota Review* 3 (Fall 1972). Copyright © 1972 by Harley Elliott. Reprinted with permission from the author.

Louise Erdrich, "Big Grass," in *Heart of the Land: Essays on Last Great Places,* ed. Joseph Barbato and Lisa Weinerman (New York: Pantheon Books, 1994), 145–50. Copyright © 1994 by Louise Erdrich. Reprinted with permission from the author.

Barbara Juster Esbensen, "Snow Print Two: Hieroglyphics," in *Cold Stars and Fireflies: Poems of the Four Seasons* (New York: Thomas Y. Crowell, 1984). Copyright © 1984 by Barbara Juster Esbensen. Reprinted with permission from HarperCollins Publishers.

Hamlin Garland, "In the Autumn Grass," in *Prairie Songs: Being Chants Rhymed and Unrhymed of the Level Lands of the Great West* (Cambridge, Mass.: Stone and Kimball, 1893), 44.

Carol Green, "Two Strangers Come to Maggie's Prairie." Copyright © 2001 by Carol Green. Printed with permission from the author.

Beverly A. J. Haley, "Tumbleweeds." Copyright © 2001 by Beverly A. J. Haley. Printed with permission from the author.

Iron Teeth, "Recollections," excerpted from "Iron Teeth, A Cheyenne Old Woman," in *The Cheyennes of Montana* by Thomas B. Marquis, ed.

Thomas D. Weist (Algonac, Mich.: Reference Publications, 1978), 52–59. Reprinted with permission from Reference Publications, Inc., Algonac, Michigan 48001–0344.

Robin E. Kelsey, "Midway Morning." Copyright © 2001 by Robin E. Kelsey. Printed with permission from the author.

William Least Heat-Moon, "Tales from Tornado Alley," excerpted from *PrairyErth (a deep map)* (Boston: Houghton Mifflin Company, 1991), 147–49. Copyright © 1991 by William Least Heat-Moon. Reprinted with permission from Houghton Mifflin Co. All rights reserved.

"The Lesson of the Birds," in *Literature Level Yellow: American Literature,* ed. Donald T. Hollenbech and Julie West Johnson (Evanston, Ill.: McDougall, Littel, 1984), 108.

Marybeth Lorbiecki, "Prairie Spirits on the Wing." Copyright © 2001 by Marybeth Lorbiecki. Printed with permission from the author.

Ann Lynn, "How to Replant a Prairie." Copyright © 2001 by Ann Lynn. Printed with permission from the author.

Walt McDonald, "Prairie Dogs Live in Lubbock," in *All That Matters: The Texas Plains in Photographs and Poems* (Lubbock: Texas Tech University Press, 1992), 91. Copyright © 1992 by Walt McDonald. Also published in *Rafting the Brazos* (1988) and *Descant* 22, no. 1 (1977). Reprinted with permission from the author.

Sheryl L. Nelms, "September in South Dakota." Copyright © 2001 by Sheryl L. Nelms. Printed with permission from the author.

Kathleen Norris, "In the Open," in *Dakota: A Spiritual Geography* (Boston: Houghton Mifflin Company, 1993), 177–79. Copyright © 1993 by Kathleen Norris. Reprinted with permission from Ticknor and Fields/Houghton Mifflin Co. All rights reserved.

Georgia O'Keeffe, "Letter from Texas," in *Lovingly, Georgia: The Complete Correspondence of Georgia O'Keeffe and Anita Pollitzer,* ed. Clive Giboire (New York: Touchstone, 1990), 183–84. Reprinted with permission from the Georgia O'Keeffe Foundation.

Cynthia Pederson, "Goldfinches" and "Migration Prayer: The Geese Speak." Copyright © 2001 by Cynthia Pederson. Printed with permission from the author.

Gary Penley, "The Blizzard," adapted from *Rivers of Wind: A Western Boyhood Remembered* (Palmer Lake, Colo.: Filter Press, 1998), 187–98. Copyright © 1998 by Gary Penley. Reprinted with permission from Filter Press.

Gillian Richardson, "Wawaskesy, the Windrunner," *Cricket* 24, no. 7 (March 1997): 47–50. Copyright © 1997 by Gillian Richardson. Reprinted with permission from *Cricket* magazine.

Cindy Rogers, "Homestead Girl." Copyright © 2001 by Cindy Rogers. Printed with permission from the author.

Patric Rowley, "The Last Best Swimming Hole," in *The Wichita Reader,* ed. Craig Miner (Wichita: Wichita Eagle and Beacon Publishing, 1996), 105–8. Copyright © 1992 by Patric Rowley. Reprinted with permission from the author.

Carl Sandburg, "Riding the Rails," excerpted from *Prairie-Town Boy* (New York: Harcourt, Brace and Company, 1952), 142–43, 145–48. Copyright © 1953, 1952 by Carl Sandburg and renewed 1981, 1980 by Margaret Sandburg, Janet Sandburg, and Helga Sandburg Crile. Reprinted with permission from Harcourt, Inc.

Nancy Sather, "Fire Crazy." Copyright © 2001 by Nancy Sather. Printed with permission from the author.

Joyce Sidman, "Ice Whales." Copyright © 2001 by Joyce Sidman. Printed with permission from the author.

Síya´ka, "Song of the Crow and Owl," in *Teton Sioux Music* by Frances Densmore, Bureau of American Ethnology Bulletin 61 (Washington, D.C.: Government Printing Office, 1918), 186.

Laurence Snydal, "Dakota Thunderstorm," in *New to North America* (Oakland, Calif.: Burning Bush Publications, 1997), 213. Copyright © 1997 by Laurence Snydal. Reprinted with permission from the author.

Elaine Terranova, "Mollie Goodnight." Copyright © 2001 by Elaine Terranova. Printed with permission from the author.

Don Welch, "How to Live in Buffalo County" in *The Point Riders: Great Plains Poetry Anthology,* ed. Frank Parman and Arn Henderson (Norman, Okla.: Point Riders Press, 1982), 57. Copyright © 1982 by Don Welch. Reprinted with permission from the author.

E. G. Willy, "Corn." Copyright © 2001 by E. G. Willy. Printed with permission from the author.

Gretchen Woelfle, "Bringing Back the Buffalo." Copyright © 2001 by Gretchen Woelfle. Printed with permission from the author.

About the Editor

Sara St. Antoine grew up in Ann Arbor, Michigan. She holds a bachelor's degree in English from Williams College and a master's degree in environmental studies from the Yale School of Forestry and Environmental Studies. Currently living in Cambridge, Massachusetts, she enjoys walking along the Charles River and seeing black-crowned night herons hunkered in the trees.

About the Illustrators

Paul Mirocha is a designer and illustrator of books about nature for children and adults. His first book, *Gathering the Desert*, by Gary Paul Nabhan, won the 1985 John Burroughs Medal for natural history. He lives in Tucson, Arizona, with his daughters, Anna and Claire.

Trudy Nicholson is an illustrator of nature with a background in medical and scientific illustration. She received her B.S. in Fine Arts at Columbia University and has worked as a natural-science illustrator in a variety of scientific fields for many years. She lives in Cabin John, Maryland.

The World As Home, the nonfiction publishing program of Milkweed Editions, is dedicated to exploring our relationship to the natural world. Not espousing any particular environmentalist or political agenda, these books are a forum for distinctive literary writing that not only alerts the reader to vital issues but offers personal testimonies to living harmoniously with other species in urban, rural, and wilderness communities.

Milkweed Editions publishes with the intention of making a humane impact on society, in the belief that literature is a transformative art uniquely able to convey the essential experiences of the human heart and spirit. To that end, Milkweed publishes distinctive voices of literary merit in handsomely designed, visually dynamic books, exploring the ethical, cultural, and esthetic issues that free societies need continually to address. Milkweed Editions is a not-for-profit press.

For more information on other books published by Milkweed Editions for intermediate readers, contact Milkweed at (800) 520-6455 or visit our website (www.milkweed.org).

Books for Middle-Grade Readers
by Milkweed Editions

Tides by V. M. Caldwell

The Ocean Within by V. M. Caldwell

The Monkey Thief by Aileen Kilgore Henderson

Treasure of Panther Peak by Aileen Kilgore Henderson

The Dog with Golden Eyes by Frances Wilbur

Join Us

Milkweed publishes adult and children's fiction, poetry, and, in its World As Home program, literary nonfiction about the natural world. Milkweed also hosts two websites: www.milkweed.org, where readers can find in-depth information about Milkweed books, authors, and programs, and www.worldashome.org, which is your online resource of books, organizations, and writings that explore ethical, esthetic, and cultural dimensions of our relationship to the natural world.

Since its genesis as *Milkweed Chronicle* in 1979, Milkweed has helped hundreds of emerging writers reach their readers. Thanks to the generosity of foundations and of individuals like you, Milkweed Editions is able to continue its nonprofit mission of publishing books chosen on the basis of literary merit—of how they impact the human heart and spirit—rather than on how they impact the bottom line. That's a miracle that our readers have made possible.

In addition to purchasing Milkweed books, you can join the growing community of Milkweed supporters. Individual contributions of any amount are both meaningful and welcome. Contact us for a Milkweed catalog or log on to www.milkweed.org and click on "About Milkweed," then "Why Join Milkweed," to find out about our donor program, or simply call (800) 520-6455 and ask about becoming one of Milkweed's contributors. As a nonprofit press, Milkweed belongs to you, the community. Milkweed's board, its staff, and especially the authors whose careers you help launch thank you for reading our books and supporting our mission in any way you can.

DATE DUE

Prin

Book

Book paper

GAYLORD   PRINTED IN U.S.A.

NORTHWEST

PACIFIC

COAST

ROCKY MOUNTAINS

TH

BOREA

GREAT

NORT

CALIFORNIA

COAST

WESTERN

DESERTS

AND

PLATEAUS

HAWAIIAN
ISLANDS